Life is lived in the borderlands – those in-bet
to navigate, but yield the greatest fruit for growth in our lives. This book will help you to travel to the next place in your spiritual journey.
Mark Batterson, New York Times *bestselling author of* The Circle Maker *and Lead Pastor, National Community Church*

This is a book for those who wonder about their lives, reflecting on meaning and purpose because they know that there is something more. And, wonderfully, it's a book about Jesus' life, and how his story releases us into the lives that we were meant to lead, but of which we might have lost sight. Full of hope for wanderers who seek something greater.
Paul Harcourt, National Leader, New Wine England

I have known Mark for many years and he is a pastoral leader of rare sensitivity; I cannot think of a better guide through the borderlands of life's changes and transitions. Rich with scripture, theological reference and personal anecdote, this book is a feast for a hungry soul, bound to bring refreshment when you most need it.
The Revd Will van der Hart, Director, Mind and Soul Foundation, and Pastoral Chaplain, Holy Trinity Brompton

Crossing borders has played a huge part of my life for two decades now. If my experience is anything to go by, it inevitably helps if you know where you are going. It also helps to have someone alongside you who can guide you and knows the way. *Borderlands* is written by someone who most definitely knows 'the way'. It is inevitable that, if you want to live a cross-shaped life, all of the issues written about here in this book with such honesty and pastoral integrity will, at some time or another, be your experience too. I deeply appreciate this book because it is full of biblical truth, wisdom words and inspiration. It is also full of hope, light and Jesus, and therefore it will help strengthen us in our long journey of adventure and obedience.
Eddie Lyle, President, Open Doors UK & Ireland

Mark Brickman has written a book about dying; dying to oneself, followed by resurrection, rising to a life of spiritual discipline. In *Borderlands*, he creates a narrative that displays the depth and breadth of his understanding of contemporary culture, the journey that brought him to seek personal 'withdrawal' from it, followed by the encounter with Jesus Christ that gave him the framework for writing the book. In twelve chapters, *Borderlands* explores, defines and espouses theories and practices, richly endowed with scriptural, literary, artistic and scholarly references, which encompass two thousand years of Christianity and offer to the followers of Christ today a challenging but encouraging guide to the life of spiritual ascent. Mark Brickman masterfully demonstrates that, for the church, there is no other path to following Christ.
Kosta Milkov, Director, RZIM Macedonia, and Founder and Director, Balkan Institute for Faith and Culture

This is a remarkable new book from a remarkable new author. It is beautifully written, brilliantly conceived, grounded in Scripture and connected to culture. Mark Brickman is a learned and gifted guide who helps the church navigate between the borderlands towards spiritual maturity in Christ. Whether you are a spiritual enquirer or a seasoned saint, there is much to thrill and teach you here. Outstanding.
Simon Ponsonby, Pastor of Theology, St Aldates, Oxford

I naively picked up this book anticipating a 'light, uplifting reflection' on Easter, only to find myself taken hold of, pulled apart and gently pieced back together in ways I did not foresee. The words flow like poetry, wrapping around you and transporting you into the paschal story as if you were experiencing those events with your own senses. I found myself lingering over sentences, reluctant to move on to the next paragraph because so much life-giving truth saturated every page. Reading this book was like a deep-tissue massage – exquisitely painful! Painful because God was working out some deep knots I hadn't even known were there. Exquisite because it was done with such a tender touch, leaving a good ache – the ache of knowing that, though it may hurt for a little while, you are going to move more freely because of it. For those stalling in their faith, this book could be a spark plug for re-ignition, as you are invited into a way of discipleship that weathers the seasons and orients you to Christ, no matter how the road bends and the landscape changes. Thank you, Mark Brickman, for writing this book.
Jo Vitale, Dean of Studies, Zacharias Institute, and Apologist, RZIM (Ravi Zacharias International Ministries)

This is a powerful and uplifting book. I was illuminated by insights from literature, psychology and spirituality, challenged afresh by the wisdom and authority of the Scriptures, and very moved by Mark Brickman's own journey of faith and discipleship. His courageous honesty is a strong thread in a pilgrimage which is both personal and universal. Anyone who sets out on this 'great adventure of spiritual growth' will be enriched in the company of such a humble and sympathetic guide who leads us along a fragrant pathway that weaves through suffering and glory, darkness and light, wilderness and wonder. We are called to self-examination, repentance and new vision, but above all we are led into the presence of the risen Christ. On finishing the book, I felt a sense of profound hope, deep joy and, in the company of Easter pilgrims throughout the ages, a new sense of destiny.
Murray Watts, writer and director, Co-founder of Riding Lights Theatre Company, screenwriter of The Miracle Maker *and Director of the arts charity The Wayfarer Trust*

Mark Brickman is Associate Minister at St Aldates in Oxford, a multi-generational church drawing many students from the city's two universities. Mark read English at the University of Cambridge, before working as a theatre and opera director for two decades. After coming to faith, he also worked as a freelance director and scriptwriter in film. His credits include *Test of Faith* (<www.testoffaith.com>), a ninety-minute documentary about science and religion. He was ordained in the Church of England in 2012.

BORDERLANDS

Mark Brickman

Navigating the Adventure of Spiritual Growth

INTER-VARSITY PRESS
36 Causton Street, London SW1P 4ST, England
Email: ivp@ivpbooks.com
Website: www.ivpbooks.com

First published 2018

British Library Cataloguing-in-Publication Data
A catalogue record for this book is available from the British Library.

ISBN: 978–1–78359–660–7
eBook ISBN: 978–1–78359–661–4

Set in 12/15 Adobe Garamond
Typeset in Great Britain by CRB Associates, Potterhanworth, Lincolnshire
Printed in Great Britain by Ashford Colour Press Ltd, Gosport, Hampshire

Inter-Varsity Press publishes Christian books that are true to the Bible and that communicate the gospel, develop discipleship and strengthen the church for its mission in the world.

IVP originated within the Inter-Varsity Fellowship, now the Universities and Colleges Christian Fellowship, a student movement connecting Christian Unions in universities and colleges throughout Great Britain, and a member movement of the International Fellowship of Evangelical Students. Website: www.uccf.org.uk. That historic association is maintained, and all senior IVP staff and committee members subscribe to the UCCF Basis of Faith.

To Jen

Contents

Foreword

It was a noisy, crowded refectory with sunlight streaming in. The place was alive with hopes and longings. At the same time there was a muddle of young children and visitors to the community wondering where to sit and what the food would be like. As a board member visiting, I had been placed opposite the head of the student body and we began a conversation. As it unfolded, I realized that I was listening to someone with a story to stop you in your tracks and the ability to tell it with haunting power.

My first meeting with Mark Brickman, described above, was unforgettable and changed our lives.

Now I believe Mark's first book, *Borderlands*, will change many lives.

Mark was a theatre director with a distinguished career behind him when he reached the borderlands of sickness with life as he knew it. He experienced what Sartre called 'nausea' (the title of his first novel) but, unlike Sartre and unlike many, Mark came to the end of himself and the beginning of life in God.

With arresting images befitting a member of the artistic community, Mark charts in this brilliantly written first book the fact that, as he puts it, 'Our culture seduces us with self-modification via retail purchase, cosmetic surgery or tabloid "seven steps" to self-improvement. Amid these temporary panaceas and continuing inner distress, the human soul aches.'

Mark is in touch with this ache of the human soul both through his own experience of it but also because he is a great listener. At that first conversation, I discovered this all too rare gift, which is in him. Because of these two gifts – experience of life and attentiveness to the stories of others – Mark is able to chart brilliantly the challenges of the human condition. Because of his Bezalel-like gift as an artist, he is able to tell them with beautiful writing. So many books are almost unreadable as a result of low artistry. Here is a new author who has high artistry and hence can move our hearts.

Later – long after our first conversation described above, at the community training him for leadership in the Church – Mark moved to Oxford with his beloved family to join our pastoral staff. He has helped me grow in faith in Christ and I believe this book will help all who read it to grow.

He has the twin capacities of always pushing the borders of where we are connecting with our city and those who live here; then, at the same time, he is dependable, deep, trustworthy and true. As well as extending community he knows how to build community in this scattered, troubled, beautiful city of dreaming spires in a truly authentic, original way: building up the body and reaching the parts others can't reach.

As such he is uniquely qualified to speak into the 'borderlands' we all find ourselves in at times. Throughout the book, he does this using a language that connects with culture yet speaks to the heart. As he says:

> As Christians, we owe it to ourselves to understand the costly relationship between human growth and suffering. The Church will never witness potently to a hurting world unless it is filled with men and women of Christlike depth who have grown through struggle.

Mark explores exactly this challenge: how to become someone who keeps on growing up to Christlikeness. If we could get hold of *that*, then there is a bright future (albeit through suffering) for the people of God in this present age.

So, sell your shirt to buy this book – and get clothed in Christlikeness instead!

Charlie Cleverly
St Aldates, Oxford

This book is about personal growth and as such is of crit
importance. Arguably what is needed in the Church is
some new self-help, seven-step programme, but a call
courage and Christlike imitation. This will take us through
borderlands of life's struggles and suffering into a new way
living for the twenty-first century. This is a book that, as M
puts it, takes us by the hand through 'the paschal account
dying and rising [which] corresponds to the many limi
passages in our lives'.

It is also a book about community. We face today a sev
challenge to the community called the Church, which,
statistics in the West are to believed, is a challenge for our ve
survival. Books appear with descriptive titles like *Disappeari
Church* or *Invisible Church*. Mark is uniquely qualified to gi
wise advice to any who love the Church and who long for h
rescue and renewal. He has been instrumental in buildi
church at the city centre of a world-class city, Oxford. H
knows the fight that there is to invent new ways of doing li
and being community.

Mark's solutions are to do with responding to God o
the journey of life. He takes us carefully and kindly on th
journey – where we are, as the chapters indicate, calle
crushed, buried, breathed on . . . then shaken, blessed, throug
longing or 'begging', as he puts it, so as to be filled, the
released and igniting others.

In his 'famous last sermon', the legendary John Stott reache
this conclusion:

> I want to share with you where my mind has come to rest as I approach the end of my pilgrimage on earth, and it is – God wants his people to become like Christ. Christlikeness is the will of God for the people of God.

Acknowledgments

My heartfelt thanks to:

David and Mary Hill, my uncle and aunt. The borderland landscape surrounding your home on the Isle of Harris in the Outer Hebrides first inspired the idea of this book.

Peronel Barnes who, in several important conversations, encouraged me to bring this project to birth.

My mother, Jenny, for pointing to the compass I needed to stop wandering and to start navigating life's borderlands more wisely.

Charlie and Anita Cleverly, Simon Ponsonby and my other gifted colleagues at St Aldates, Oxford. I learn more from you all than I can say.

Steve Mitchell, my editor at IVP, who first responded to the manuscript. Your judicious eye and encouragement helped me greatly in the rewriting.

Rima Devereaux and her colleagues at IVP, for refining the manuscript further and delivering it in beautiful book form.

Andrew Miller, for your generous proofreading and fierce attention to detail.

All those who kindly offered commendations. For these, much thanks.

Jen, Fin and Skye. For your patience when this book clawed for my attention, and for your faithful and tender championing of it.

'There is a divine element in humankind –
an element which no tomb can imprison.'
F. W. Boreham[1]

'Who would have thought my shriveled heart
Could have recovered greenness?'
George Herbert, 'The Flower'[2]

1
Introduction

The spectral figure stands, newly risen from the tomb. His upright body is wrapped in grave clothes. He shuffles towards life but his head rolls back exhausted on one shoulder, eyelids sealed. It tilts back to the tomb, as if still caught in sleep. The figure recalls a moth, unable to break free from its chrysalis. This is sculptor Jacob Epstein's *Lazarus*, situated in the foyer of New College chapel, Oxford.[3] Fashioned in the wake of the death of the sculptor's wife and the wearied aftermath of the Second World War, this mesmeric sculpture stands as a type for our modern age. Epstein's artistic insight, in depicting the head turned back, is to suggest that, for all our desire for growth, we often remain locked in confining patterns of past thinking. Growing and maturing challenge us. In that sense, the sculpture speaks of the human condition. It also, importantly, speaks of much contemporary spirituality. In the figure's solitariness (no Christ stands before it, no community bustles around it), it embodies an isolated faith and a diminished understanding that even Christian believers can have about spiritual growth. We need to move beyond this figure's solitude and stasis.

For many people in our culture, growth and change are real struggles for which our educational system and elders fail to prepare us. Equally for Christians, growth can be something that we prefer to avoid. For all that our culture vaunts personal change, we know that its cost is usually suffering and pain. It is not easy passing from one life stage to another or dealing with the violence of job loss, bankruptcy, depression or bereavement. Involuntary change comes at a price, and it is no different with spiritual change and growth that we voluntarily seek. To die to our existing identity and allow another to emerge is profoundly challenging, as Epstein's sculpture intimates. Yet grappling with suffering and change is intrinsic to mature spirituality. Jesus' project is to bring vitalizing new life, even if renewal comes at a cost. As he pithily observed, it is only when a grain of wheat falls to the ground and dies that it bears fruit.

As Christians, we owe it to ourselves to understand the costly relationship between human growth and suffering. The Church will never witness potently to a hurting world unless it is filled with men and women of Christlike depth who have grown through struggle. Our culture seduces us with self-modification via retail purchase, cosmetic surgery or tabloid 'seven steps' to self-improvement. Amid these temporary panaceas and continuing inner distress, the human soul aches. Christianity, by contrast, offers a rich, deep path of discipleship. In following Jesus, we better understand and process our suffering, we grow and discover fullness of life 'in Christ'. This book is for anyone who wants to embrace that fullness of life, albeit at a cost.

William Bridges, an expert on human transitions, describes how people experiencing personal change in contemporary culture often drift in 'an unritualized life-passage'.[4] By this, he means a process not held within any larger container of meaning or supported by others. Our ritual-free culture equips us little for such crossings. This was my experience in my twenties and thirties when, as an agnostic, I was psychologically wounded, spiritually hungry and looking for answers in all the wrong places. I was caught up in a process of transition that I did not understand. School and university had taught me nothing about life stages or working with suffering. I'd scan self-help bookshelves for hours, try one therapy after another, flirt with any form of spirituality under the sun, but without any achieved understanding of the change process in which I was caught. Bridges sees this lack of meaningful story as fundamental to our contemporary plight about personal change:

> It is not the fact of being in transition that most people mind, but rather that they cannot place their experience of being in transition within any larger, meaningful context. Without such a context, the endings are for no reason, the beginnings open the door to nowhere, and the neutral zones extend end-to-end across an empty landscape.[5]

Stranded in this bleak cultural territory, my life felt confusing for far too long. Bereavement, depression and failure overwhelmed me. I stood without adequate map or navigating tools. It was a place of spiritual openness, because I was acutely aware of my own insufficiency, but a place without answers or anchors – what anthropologists who study personal growth call a place of 'liminality' or transition. In such borderlands, or in-between places, we find control wrenched from our hands. God calls men and women into such territory throughout the pages of Scripture, so as to become receptive to new formation. Ultimately nurturing, such landscapes are frequently disorienting and baffling at first. We need the right map to navigate them. Equipped with one, we discover that suffering invites us into fruitful change. We no longer feel lost. Accepting God's invitation, we release the past and open ourselves to new, emerging realities. We learn, engage creatively with a shifting present, and experience growth. The writer of Hebrews describes this as running 'the race marked out for us' (12:1). The landscape may appear at times opaque, as if we career through mist across craggy fells. However, we do not run into a hopeless unknown. We fix our eyes on the one bearing this invitation, Jesus, 'the author and perfecter of our faith' (12:2). In his suffering, death and resurrection, he models a spiritual mystery into which we can enter and through which we grow.

This book describes the unending mystery of identifying with Christ. It is not an easy process even for Christians to accept. Evangelicalism (my tradition) affirms conversion through personal surrender in faith to Jesus. Evangelicals often have a less developed language for mature discipleship of personal identification with Christ. One of the most helpful models on which we can draw is the great fifty days of Easter. This expands the time frame of the Catholic model of the 'paschal mystery' – the movement through Christ's suffering, death and resurrection to his ascension. The fifty days helpfully includes Pentecost and the Spirit's outpouring. These two narratives (paschal mystery and fifty days) depict the deepest human drama that any person can undergo; the cycle in which we discover the love of God in our suffering; the mystery through which, via Calvary's narrow door, wider life floods in. They chart a spiritual transition from deepest darkness to glorious light. Our future death lies traced in their contours. Yet they also describe the many smaller deaths and risings that we pass through in life. As such, they can speak to us much about our spiritual growth and daily discipleship. This book enlarges the picture frame still further to encompass Gethsemane and the road to Calvary, as well as the early church's emergence in the book of Acts. This is because my strategy is to track Jesus' disciples through this entire period. For me, their spiritual growth is perfectly imaged in the contrast between their fearful scattering at Gethsemane and their fruitful scattering from Jerusalem to spread the gospel, following Stephen's death.

Ronald Rolheiser's spirituality of the paschal mystery in his book *The Holy Longing* has been a strong influence.[6] While I do not agree with all of Rolheiser's theology, as with other Catholic authors whom I quote, he offers a poetic summary of the paschal events which I have found illuminating. My own treatment is more rooted in robust exposition of the gospel narratives of Jesus' death and resurrection, partly out of a desire for evangelical rigour and partly because I believe there are further nuances of understanding to be mined from the Christological nature of events. The next ten chapters therefore closely detail events from Gethsemane to Stephen's martyrdom. They aim to draw the reader into each stage of personal change. For a broader, more panoramic perspective, the reader will have to await the book's final chapter where, through Jesus' lived example, I explore what primary virtue might be most helpful to cultivate in our navigating spiritual growth.

Doctrinal exposition and narrative theology will both be germane in my process. Early in his ministry, Jesus addresses the Jewish authorities persecuting him:

> You diligently study the Scriptures because you think that by them you possess eternal life. These are the Scriptures that testify

> about me, yet you refuse to come to me to have life . . . If you believed Moses, you would believe me, for he wrote about me. (John 5:39–40, 46)

Jesus' Jewish disciples were steeped in these Scriptures. He will further expand their doctrinal understanding after his resurrection when he unpacks Old Testament Scripture afresh and shows himself prefigured there. However, the disciples' narrative from Gethsemane to the book of Acts is also one of lived experience. There can be real benefits in studying their very human journey through this period. Despite receiving a first-class theological education from their master, they struggle between Gethsemane and the ascension, as we often do too in times of change, despite our theological knowledge. Writers on change often glibly compare change with the metamorphosis of a caterpillar to a butterfly. That process, though, is, in biological practice, less graceful than messy and convulsive:

> We have not much language to appreciate this phase of decay, this withdrawal, this era of ending that must precede beginning. Nor of the violence of the metamorphosis, which is often spoken of as though it were as graceful as a flower blooming.[7]

Contemporary Christians need a descriptive account of change that is realistic about its often ungainly processes. Otherwise we hold up impossibly high standards to ourselves and never maturely deal with spiritual change. We find such an account in the great fifty days narrative. 'Stories are just data with a soul,' asserts Brenee Brown.[8] The gospel stories chime with our soul in times of transformation. To paraphrase William Bridges, they place our experience of being in transition within the largest, meaningful context available to us as Christians.

At the same time, we can learn from insights in other poetic, contemplative and mythic traditions. Thus this book complements its exposition of the New Testament narratives with material from literary, psychological and anthropological sources. The insights offered by these traditions can further stretch our understanding, inspire our empathy and stimulate our imagination. They can help to get us deeper into the human drama portrayed.

Nevertheless, for all this book's cross-disciplinary method, my conviction is that such insights from other traditions remain partial until they find their fulfilment in Christianity. No story from secular tradition can reach deep enough into our belief structure to change us, compared with the transformative power of Jesus' death and rising. Each of the stages of change in the events that I describe revolves around a single axis, the unique person of Jesus Christ. He stands at the centre of the paschal events and, as we enter this cycle more fully, we enter more fully into him. For any reader wanting to explore a complementary approach to this book, Ignatius' Spiritual Exercises provide a rich contemplative path to the same goal.

This journey of identification and discovery will resonate for us in any personal season of change. It is also, though, a lifelong journey. The paschal account of dying and rising corresponds to the many liminal passages in our lives. It also points forward to our physical death and the bodily resurrection promised us in eternity. Requiring our cooperating powers, it remains a quintessentially mysterious process, as Paul suggests with his two metaphors of birth (Galatians 4:19) and chrysalis transformation (Romans 12:2). We are human agents but embedded in a larger cyclical process. In that sense, it is the deepest of mysteries and one that no single book can fathom. Nevertheless, I write in trust that these gospel events provide a definitive answer to contemporary culture's questions while offering vital communal lessons for us as believers. My experience of profound transition in early adulthood was bewildering because I lacked any meaningful context in which to understand it. However, it was also disorienting because it was a journey that I made alone. Liminal change is always best when experienced in community, as it was by Jesus' disciples.

For myself, coming to faith in Christ was transformative. I no longer lingered on life's edge, like Epstein's spectral figure. At last I was surrounded by a community of people of shared belief with whom I could travel. I had a coherent world view that explained my years of painful transition. Most sweetly, I had discovered and entered a redeeming relationship with Jesus Christ. The question now was how to progress in this relationship and what it would mean for the rest of my life. The answer lies in the mystery of Jesus' incarnation, suffering, death and resurrection. Identifying with Christ in these, we experience spiritual formation, step into renewed life and share in his sufferings and glory. Living into this life through contemplation and prayer, we are drawn into a deeper experience of, and more intimate union with, God. Moreover, this process is one not just of personal spiritual growth but also of collective renewal. The disciples' new lives, as well as that of the early church, were birthed from the events of the fifty-day cycle. Its implications remain as vital for us today.

*'There are some things so dear, some things so precious,
some things so eternally true, that they are worth dying for.
And I submit to you that if a man has not discovered
something that he will die for, he isn't fit to live.'*
Martin Luther King[1]

*'The Gethsemane experience came in the dark season.
It came when Jesus was alone . . . No one goes with you
in Gethsemane. You decide to surrender. You decide
to embrace the plans and the will of the Father.'*
Ingrid Hansen[2]

2

Called

Our Christian life begins long before our arrival in Gethsemane. It commences with God's call on our lives. Until we reach Gethsemane's borderlands, we have freely responded to God's loving invitation. His call has likely come to us in double fashion: first, as a revelation that Jesus is Lord; second, as an invitation to a particular life work. This second call of God on our lives comes in different ways. We may discover it as we faithfully follow our personal desires. We may discover it as we respond to the world's deep hunger. Life crisis, such as breakdown, redundancy, illness or failure, can create a demanding new context. We discover call in seeking to find God's meaning in our situation. Whatever, though, there is always a duality to God's calling. We see this imaged in the angel's visit to a young girl who learns she will carry the longed-for Messiah in her womb. This visitation fulfils Mary's profoundest longings for a child and to serve God. It also comes as a sword to her heart, foreshadowing the day in which she will huddle beneath a bloody cross on which her adult son will hang in agony to save the world. Desire, death and future fruit all converge in this visitation, anticipating the night stage of any calling – that place called Gethsemane.

Gethsemane is a place where call converges with crisis. It is where our commitment to follow as disciples carries us into deeper water than we would like. It is the dark place where we arrive again and again in our Christian walk. Here the cost of following Jesus is starkly revealed. Here too a fog of confusion can descend. Gethsemane is the first of our borderlands, or threshold places. John O'Donohue observes that the etymology of the word 'threshold' involves 'threshing', with its separation of grain from husk.[3] Thresholds are life stages that 'thresh' our desires, character and purpose. In the Christian story, the call to inner transformation and future fruit begins with a grain of wheat falling to the ground and dying. Transformation comes through suffering: this is the Gethsemane lesson that the disciples fail to grasp. In such a crucible, events coalesce around a single, demanding question: are we prepared to die (usually metaphorically, occasionally literally) for the thing for which we have long desired? Martin Luther King challenged his listeners with this very question in his speech in Detroit back in 1963. Hearing these words as an agnostic at a midnight Christmas Eve service two years before coming to faith, I had to ask myself if I knew either what I was prepared to die for or, singularly, what I was therefore living for. It was my stunned inability to answer either question that drew me into a weekly return to church, although it would be another eighteen months and in a different church before I heard the good news of Jesus Christ clearly proclaimed.

Jesus' most provocative challenge to us is to die daily. This concept can seem utter folly to the world. What on earth has dying to self got to do with the big throbbing heart of this thing called life? Yet the paradox embedded at the heart of the great fifty days is that any journey into deeper life will always involve a progressive death to self. We see this rigorously played out in Gethsemane. Here Jesus elects to journey to the cross and through death in order to effect God's saving work for humankind. This is the point where any disciple's calling and continuing commitment can threaten to become uncoupled. Here Jesus himself sweats blood and trembles, petitioning his Father in case there just might be another way.

It's worth asking ourselves how calling has functioned similarly in our lives. To what degree has calling been attractive, alluring, forbidding or even a thing of terror? For many years in my twenties and thirties, I was a young man fuelled by creative desire. My desire led me squarely into twenty years of theatre directing. This was my vocation, one married to personal passion and a sufficient modicum of creative talent. Some years later I became a Christian. Now calling showed another face. After several years of Christian faith, I travelled to a retreat centre to pray to God and ask whether he was calling me to ordination, something of which I had felt an intimation, somewhat to my horror, a few weeks before. At the end of a day in which I had failed to hear the still small voice of God, it was a shock, as I was ending a labyrinth prayer walk in a mown field, to hear God say to me of this potential call, 'Commit, and the passion will come later.' What a foreign idea of calling to my soul! Yet what a necessary corrective to the idea of vocation uncomplicatedly tied to personal longing. Looking back on my younger self, a youth driven by creative desire, I can now see that God was asking me to reframe my understanding of calling. This did not make the next eighteen months of testing this calling easy (the passion was very much to come later in the process). It did, though, provide me with a compass and a trust that I needed to allow passion to emerge over time. I should not expect it smartly to stand to attention at a drumbeat.

One turning point late in this process came on my receiving an email from Charlie Cleverly, rector of St Aldates, where I would serve my curacy after two years of theological training. I had emailed Charlie before starting in post to ask if he'd be happy for me to continue my link to a secular organization that I'd formerly worked for in London, creating training workshops for young professionals hungry for meaning and purpose. No, he replied, he did not think this would be helpful:

> If it is any consolation, when you get ordained it is like a death. I remember that 'diamond of an Elizabethan', Edmund Campion, when getting ordained, saying: he felt as 'one just embarking from the world, in some sort a dying man . . . I went to my rest in the sepulcher of the Church' . . . While we don't have quite such a high view as him, there is a death – but if we are prepared to die, we then find life from the dead.

I knew instinctively that Charlie was right. But it was another death knell in my journey of calling. Why embrace such calling, then? Quite simply, because at such moments in life an inner conviction tells us that it is impossible not to follow this path. Calling may not always be a work that we salivate to do. It can be a call to which we simply are unable to say 'No'. Whether one regards it as coming from an existential sense of rightness, the pull of a deeper current beneath the surface waters of life or the personal leading of Jesus Christ, refusal becomes impossible. Having sweated blood, we say 'Yes', despite every inclination of our heart. We grasp on to the joy set before us, even as the shoreline of our former life collapses, eroded by pounding waves. This is the Gethsemane moment. Let us examine it further in Scripture.

The motif of wrestling marks our experience in Gethsemane. This garden is a place of testing and struggle, ultimately with God. It's interesting to consider that after the tenderly communal evening of the Last Supper, Gethsemane should so shockingly involve Christ's isolation. Dying to self is always a desert experience. As Ingrid Hansen observes, 'no one goes with you in Gethsemane.'[4] In one sense, Jesus' three closest friends, the ones who shared in his transfiguration, are only metres from his side. Yet they could be on the other side of the world, so existentially alone is he and so racked with fatigue are they. In the title of a Maggi Hambling painting depicting a tiny solitary figure tramping across the vast expanse of a circus ring, *The Search Is Always Alone*.

After the time of intimacy in the upper room comes the time of greatest testing, a time in which Satan is very much present. This enemy lurks in Gethsemane's shadows, as the opening scene of Mel Gibson's film *The Passion* memorably evokes. This is a territory in which calling balances on a knife edge, made or marred through prayer. It is only in prayer that Jesus can find the new language to confront his situation. He prays with an intensity that we've never seen before, throwing himself down headlong, uttering deep cries to his Father, literally sweating blood. Is it any wonder that only prayer, the instrument of faith by which we interact with God, can offer adequate compass in this fearsome territory? For as the theologian Belden Lane observes in his study of desert spirituality, 'The desert is where one confronts one's inevitable loss of control, the inadequacy of language, the spectre of one's own demise.'[5] We now have to understand all these actual or potential losses within a larger perspective that only God can provide. In this place where the wild things are, as at the time of Christ's desert temptation, both devil and ministering angels roam. How could both not be present when what is at stake is not just personal dissolution but the redemption of the cosmos? What, then, can we learn from Jesus' prayerful example? What lessons for us lie in his wrestling and his assent to walk the flint-strewn way to the cross?

As commentators have long noted, Gethsemane means 'oil press' and may have been the enclosed olive orchard preserved at the base of the Mount of Olives today. It is the place where Jesus agrees to be crushed through his love for each one of us. Sweating blood, being squeezed in the oil press: the imagery is of allowing everything in us to be crushed so that a harvest of oil can be reaped. Although in one sense this crushing is a horror, in another it speaks of a larger, unimaginably generous love. Ultimately, Jesus can stand in this place and stand strong because he knows that in the cross lies the fulfilment of God's deepest plan. The same love that sent Jesus into this world to die for it will lift him from the grave, bring new life through his resurrection and raise him to the Father's right hand, releasing the coming of the Holy Spirit for all people on earth. In the words of Ingrid Hansen, 'When we fully say, "Abba! Father! All things are possible for You; remove this cup from Me; yet not what I will, but what you will" (Mark 14:35–36), oil can come from our lives and be used to touch the people around us.'[6] Our personal Gethsemanes invite us to look beyond our immediate context, to remember Christ's death and resurrection, and to have confidence in the coming new life. In this way, dying to self isn't terminal but liminal, a place of threshing, a narrow doorway opening to a wider, open space.

The psychology of Gethsemane is one where arduous wrestling yields to surrender and consecration. If we wish to prepare for such threshold moments in our lives, this is the dynamic that we need to court in our inner work. There is a parallel here with the experience of people caught up in life-threatening survival situations. John Leach, a psychologist expert in this area, describes how successful survivors are marked by their ability to be active or passive in a time of crisis, depending on what is required at each moment:

> Complete passiveness leads to subjection, apathy and usually death. An inability to accept one's condition leads to frustration, anger and irrational behaviour, again often followed by death . . . The key factor here is *knowing* when to be active and when to be passive and the realization that passivity is itself a deliberate and 'active' act.[7]

This perfectly describes the shift from Jesus' active wrestling to his profound surrender to his Father's call. Such active passiveness will be the hallmark of his passion, that word itself carrying the meaning of submission and surrender. His walk to the cross is neither vigorously active (how could it be when he is about to be stripped, whipped, scourged and brutally nailed to wood?) nor hopelessly passive (impossible when he has willingly acceded to his Father's will in prayer). Instead, Jesus, in his humility, elects to embrace suffering and death for our wrongdoing. Scripture images his assent with a metaphorical action and a prayer. He lifts the cup of suffering to his lips and prays, 'yet not my will, but yours be done' (Luke 22:42).

When we accept this kind of sword to our hearts, when we become this grain splitting so that new life might come, in our time of greatest trial God sends ministering angels to our side (Luke 22:43). In our paschal narrative, there will be angels here, later at the tomb and finally at Christ's ascension. There will be no more angels from that point on, even at Pentecost. But Gethsemane is a time of supernatural crisis when heavenly agents strengthen Jesus against demonic temptation. Revived, he cries, 'Rise, let us go!' (Matthew 26:46) and walks forward, in acceptance, to his bloody calling.

It is worth considering what such a Gethsemane experience looks like in more contemporary form. Douglas Brown was a Baptist minister from Balham, London, who became a catalyst in the East Anglian Revival of 1921. Christians in Lowestoft had been praying for revival for two years when Brown arrived one March day to begin a week's mission. As a result of his preaching and teaching, a great awakening began, spreading to other coastal towns and even north-east Scotland after Scottish herring fishermen returned there from their summer work in East Anglian ports. In the first eleven weeks of this East Anglian revival, one thousand people surrendered their lives to Christ. The revival is heralded as the last significant twentieth-century revival on English soil. Yet Brown had to go through his own oil-press experience before he could be part of this harvest.

By Brown's own testimony, his Gethsemane visitation began one evening in October 1920, four months before going to Lowestoft for the mission: 'God laid hold of me in the midst of a Sunday evening service and nearly broke my heart while I was preaching.'[8] The experience came amid a happy period of his tenure littered with weekly conversions. Initially Brown recounts that he did not know why he was broken-hearted. However, later that night, shut away from his wife in his study, 'Christ laid his hand on a proud minister, and told him that he had not gone far enough, that there were reservations in his surrender, and He wanted him to do a piece of work that he had been trying to evade.' Brown adds, 'I knew what He meant.'[9] God's call, then, was unwelcome, indeed repugnant, to this disciple. So began Brown's bloody wrestling with God.

While Christ's Gethsemane takes place within the almost inconceivable compass of one hour, Brown's extended over four months. So it is often with us. Our Gethsemane experiences tend to be rather more protracted than Christ's, such is our tendency for denial and evasion. Brown fully understood his call but 'was not prepared to pay the price'.[10] There is a price indeed for such a call. As Brown's struggle continued through November and Christmas of 1920, his prideful ego assaulted him with visions of humility, picturing him on his knees before his congregation:

> The struggle went on, and I said to the Lord, 'You know that it is not my work. I will pray for anyone else who does it, but please do not give it to me, it will kill me. I cannot get into the pulpit and plead with people. It is against my temperament, and You made me.'[11]

Unlike Jesus' dark night of the soul, there is almost something comical about Brown's infuriated protestations. He pleads his temperament (God's own handiwork!). He refutes his situation. Meanwhile, he remains locked in ardent struggle with God, like Jacob wrestling, refusing the cup that he has been offered. Only after his Gethsemane had ended was Brown ruefully able to admit: 'I thought that what was wrong was my circumstances, when what was really wrong was Douglas Brown. We always put it down to our circumstances as long as we can.'[12] Retrospectively he was able to admit his own reservedness and pride. At the time, though, all he experienced was confusion, indignation and contempt. We cannot underestimate his personal pain.

Presented as an almost satirical self-portrait of ministerial pride, Brown's testimony is drawn in lighter hues than the Gospels' tortured depiction of Jesus' garden agony. Yet they share many elements: the existential solitude of the individual caught in his Gethsemane, the prayerful wrestling with God and the intensity of a spiritual night journey across a stormy ocean. In contrast to Jesus' surrender in humility after a single hour, Brown remained wilfully active, refusing surrender to God's call. Even he, though, finally acceded to God's mission and strode forth from his crucible. We will have to leave it until a later chapter to see exactly what caused his wrestling to cease.

Gethsemane humbles us. It forces the addict in us to admit our life is out of control. It forces the narcissist in us to own our pride. Whatever our Achilles heel or inveterate sin, Gethsemane summons us to the way of humility. Humbly Jesus bows his will to walk the way of the cross. Sadly, humility is often regarded as a lesser spiritual virtue in a world that demands assertion and high-performance impact. The Antarctic explorer Captain Scott noted his own observations on this point in a letter written from his hut at Cape Evans:

> Under ordinary conditions it is so easy to carry a point with a little bounce; self-assertion is a mask which covers many a weakness. As a rule we have neither the time nor the desire to look beneath it, and so it is that we commonly accept people on their own valuation. Here the outward show is nothing, it is the inward purpose that counts. So the 'Gods' dwindle and the humble supplant them. Pretence is useless.[13]

Scott was talking about how the golden boys that he had employed for his expedition so often faltered in crises compared with their humbler and less outwardly impressive teammates. In Gethsemane, the 'Gods' among the disciples, with their previously loud protestations of fidelity, dwindle. In this place, there is an unrobing of false pretence. True character is laid bare. Humility also brings with it clear reflection, unlike the sea-tossed thinking of Douglas Brown during his four months in the oil press. We can contrast Brown's feverish wrestling with the steadier lucidity of Dietrich Bonhoeffer, whose Gethsemane lasted only a single month.

Bonhoeffer, who would go to his death in Nazi Germany at the hands of Hitler's servants, had travelled to New York to teach in June 1939. Feted by American Christians, he returned to Germany less than one month later. Although this period in America was a soul-searching one, contrast Brown's egotistic independence and impertinent struggles with God with Bonhoeffer's steady focus on God's will and his refusal to choose a life of exiled security:

> I have had the time to think and to pray about my situation and that of my nation and to have God's will for me clarified. I have come to the conclusion that I have made a mistake in coming to America. I must live through this difficult period of our national history with the Christian people of Germany. I shall have no right to participate in the reconstruction of Christian life in Germany after the war if I do not share the trials of this time with my people . . . Christians in Germany will face the terrible alternative of either willing the defeat of their nation in order that Christian civilization may survive, or willing the victory of their nation, and thereby destroying our civilization. I know which of these alternatives I must choose, but I cannot make that choice in security.[14]

Brown is immersed in his own ego struggles. Bonhoeffer cannot refuse the call to participate in his people's sufferings and destiny. Their perspectives differ, accounting for their different times in the desert, yet observe that God graciously uses both men in powerful ways once their wrestling is over. God has no favourites. Brown's legacy in revival is as remarkable, in its way, as Bonhoeffer's was on a more public stage.

What steadiness and resolve can we learn from Bonhoeffer? One answer lies in a diary entry recorded shortly before his decision to return to Germany. He had just read Paul's petition to Timothy to 'get here before winter' (2 Timothy 4:21). Bonhoeffer resonates with Paul's plea, fearing a time that might otherwise be too late:

> It is for us as for soldiers, who come home on leave from the front but who, in spite of all their expectations, long to be back at the front again. We cannot get away from it any more. Not because we are necessary, or because we are useful (to God?), but simply because that is where our life is, and because we leave our life behind, destroy it, if we cannot be in the midst of it again. It is nothing pious, more like some vital urge. But God acts not only by means of pious emotions, but also through vital ones.[15]

I have seldom read a more profound definition of calling. Bonhoeffer defines his need to return to the frontline of spiritual struggle not as a matter of necessity or pious desire to be God's instrument but simply as a 'vital urge'. Bonhoeffer could not but return. For all the pain that it will bring him, it causes him greater pain to be away from the fray. So we too can meditate on 'getting there before winter', embracing our heart's cause before obstacles intensify. This is not dutifulness but a matter of integrity of soul.

Hellmut Traub recalls seeing Bonhoeffer on his unexpected return from America. While Traub comments that, objectively, Bonhoeffer had returned to 'dismal slavery and a dark future', he perceived a man totally faithful to his own reality.[16] Traub wrote that this 'gave to everything he told us then a strong and joyful firmness, such as only arises out of realized freedom'.[17] Bonhoeffer 'knew he had taken a clear step, though the actualities before him were still quite unclear'.[18] Pressed, his oil could flow. Christ's example is not impossible. Bonhoeffer walked, clear-eyed, towards his calling.

As a prelude to scrutinizing the disciples' more flawed response to Christ's call, we need to consider how human beings can wilfully refuse a personal Gethsemane. If Gethsemane represents a threshold, a required rite of passage, it is, of course, entirely possible to turn away from such a rite. We can do so through wilful independence, immaturity or lack of resources to traverse this alarming threshold. I want to linger briefly over a literary work that brilliantly anatomizes such a failure. Ian McEwan's novella *On Chesil Beach* describes the wedding night of a young couple, Edward and Florence, in a Dorset hotel in 1962. Initially, the evening is marked by a sense of giddy excitement that we recognize from the new horizons in our own lives: 'Almost strangers, they stood, strangely together, on a new pinnacle of existence, gleeful that their new status promised to promote them out of their endless youth – Edward and Florence, free at last!'[19] Rapidly, though, they become prey to internal turmoil, the young man insecure about his sexual prowess and the possibly abused young woman afraid of imminent sexual surrender. There are also larger cultural forces at work:

> And what stood in their way? Their personalities and pasts, their ignorance and fear, timidity, squeamishness, lack of entitlement or experience or easy manners, then the tail end of a religious prohibition, their Englishness and class, and history itself. Nothing much at all.[20]

The duo is inadequately prepared both personally and culturally for crossing the threshold of marriage. They need a much larger story to inhabit than they currently do. In the face of such obstacles, they risk botching this threshold, retreating in fear or succumbing to selfish desire. So it is that when Edward prematurely ejaculates in a flurry of rising desire, each proves inadequate to negotiate this difficulty. Florence flees their hotel to the shingle of Chesil Beach, pursued by her angry and confused beau:

> Whatever conversation they were about to have, she dreaded it. As she understood it, there were no words to name what had happened, there existed no shared language in which two adults could describe such events to each other. And to argue about it was even further beyond her imagining. There could be no discussion . . . The matter lay between them, as solid as a geographical feature, a mountain, a headland. Unnameable, unavoidable. And she was ashamed.[21]

This is frightening territory. Gethsemane is a borderland, terrifying at times but still a territory through which one can travel. But here there is only headland, fixed and immovable. The longed-for goal of marital union is eclipsed; all that the two young people can see is shame and failure.

McEwan brilliantly captures key elements of this kind of marred threshold: denial and avoidance of that which needs to be discussed; an inability to hold a larger conversation that embraces new challenges and issues of sacrifice and self-restraint; a narrowing of imagination so that the mind becomes confined to the bungled moment in the bedroom, endlessly recapitulating its humiliations; a sense of shame at being inadequate to the task of mutual forgiveness. Contrast this with Paul's exhortation to us in Hebrews 12:2 to run the race marked out for us and to 'fix our eyes on Jesus, the author and perfecter of our faith, who for the joy set before him endured the cross'. Only through fixing our eyes on such a goal can we turn our eyes from within ourselves and find resources to steer through liminal territory.

It is worth noting that Jesus' principal tool in this territory is prayer, also that he here plumbs a new range of expression in his prayers to God. Thus, he is described as 'deeply distressed and troubled' (Mark 14:33) and 'overwhelmed with sorrow to the point of death' (v. 34). Matthew's Gospel tells us that Jesus falls with his face to the ground to pray (26:39). Rites of passage always invite us to name our situation with a larger language than we've formerly known. Jesus discovers this language *in extremis*, doubtless groaning in his Spirit as he sweats blood in prayer. The disciples, on the other hand, fall asleep in exhausted confusion. They fail to enter into a wider conversation with God. So it is that they will end up marooned after fleeing Gethsemane, having botched this threshold, covered in shame and regret.

McEwan's drama ends with Florence fleeing Edward on Chesil Beach, wounded by his words of acrimony and accusation. Yet the narrator clarifies that she would have turned back had Edward uttered kind words. This threshold could have been crossed:

> All she had needed was the certainty of his love, and his reassurance that there was no hurry when a lifetime lay ahead of them. Love and patience – if only he had had them both at once – would surely have seen them through. And then what unborn children might have had their chances, what young girl with an Alice band might have become his loved familiar? This is how the entire course of a life can be changed – by doing nothing.[22]

Here again are vital clues to a successful negotiation of our Gethsemanes. We require strength of heart, a clear goal, and an ability to wait in patience rather than to demand impossibly swift resolution of our difficulty. We need to give voice to our tenderest aspirations of heart instead of standing 'in cold and righteous silence'.[23] In short, we must give up our self-absorbed pain, dying to it, accepting a deeper call that requires the beginnings of new maturity. Without responding in this way, we are condemned to regret, as McEwan pinpoints when he describes Edward's response later in life to reading a review of Florence's performance in a concert: 'At last he could admit to himself that he had never met anyone he loved as much, that he had never found anyone, man or woman, who matched her seriousness.'[24] Edward is haunted, part of him still marooned in the garden of lovers. At last he can see the consequences of his refusal to be crushed in Gethsemane's oil press. It is a fate that we should wish on no-one.

We come finally to the disciples' behaviour in Gethsemane, as their flawed human responses offer vital lessons for our discipleship. At one level, their sleeping as Jesus prays suggests a kind of denial. It is as if they cannot bear their confusion about their master's motives. Visiting Jerusalem recently, it was intriguing to visit the cave situated close to Gethsemane where, it is conjectured at least, the disciples may have sought refuge and slept as Jesus prayed. This cave setting suggests a kind of willed entry into darkness and unconsciousness. By contrast, the nearby Church of the Agony adjoining the Gethsemane garden contains a section of bedrock around its altar where Jesus allegedly prayed before his arrest. Approaching the low stone wall bordering this area, I was startled to see pilgrims previously concealed crouched around this rock. Heads bowed, they were praying their own Gethsemane prayers, perhaps in relation to cups that God was inviting them to drink. The cave and the rock: settings of denial and trial.

The disciples' sleeping reminds me of times of denial in my own life. I think of a desperate time of struggle when I was running a northern regional theatre, engulfed by the need to escape. As I stood alone in a lift one day ascending to our rehearsal room, I remember thinking – perhaps if I pretend to faint and the actors find me when these doors open, I will be signed off as ill and be able to escape this whole sorry mess. I never did stage that fainting fit but it was only a few months later that I resigned and left my post. I fled, as the disciples do, and returned to my London flat. Here I sat and ate ashes for several months, struggling to comprehend what had happened. My recovery and movement into new life took much, much longer.

Beyond their sleep of denial, the disciples fail their Gethsemane trial because they misunderstand Jesus' mission and method. Assuming his earlier triumphal entry into Jerusalem to signal imminent victory over Roman conquerors, they cannot accept the prospect of surrender in the garden. They behave as if there is a way of avoiding the cross (dying to self) by martial force. Peter draws his sword on the high priest's servant, for example, severing his ear. With Jesus arrested the disciples see only loss, humiliation and defeat. Their dream has proved illusory. They flee to save their skins. At core this is a crisis of understanding and faith. We need both to sustain us in our Gethsemanes. Imperfect in our understanding of the deeper call on our lives, we too easily embrace self-willed, independent action. We refuse to be crushed. No oil can then flow from our lives to bring blessing to others.

Sacrifice has been described as a healthy denial, 'denying ourselves something we want for the sake of something we want even *more*'.[25] For the disciples, that 'something we want even more' has suddenly vanished. They sought messianic victory, not the humiliating arrest of a leader who seems only intent on prayer, summons no armies of angels and rebukes their taking up of arms. Viewed in isolation, a Gethsemane will always be meaningless, a defeat. Only understood in the context of the paschal narrative does it become a crucible for transformation. So the disciples flee the garden in panic when they might have embraced breakthrough to God's deeper, life-giving call.

I want to consider one final anthropological dynamic to the disciples' failure in Gethsemane. Scholars point out that in Jewish tradition a young man would disciple himself to a rabbi while between the ages of twelve and thirty. It is entirely likely that the disciples were young men below the age of thirty, some possibly even teenagers, when they chose to follow Jesus. John Leach, survival psychologist, observes that the primary age for adaptation and long-term survival in life-threatening crises appears to be between twenty-five and thirty-five:

> Those under twenty-five suffer because they have not yet learned to conserve their energies. They have difficulty pacing themselves for the long haul of survival and consequently burn themselves out in the beginning. A key characteristic of long-term survivors is active-passiveness, and passiveness does not come naturally to youth.[26]

As it is anthropologically, so it is spiritually. Consider, given the likely youth of the disciples, how challenging Gethsemane and its aftermath must have been for them. As youths, we are fired up by eros, personal desire and intense hunger for life. Young male adulthood is all about tearing up roots, leaving home and making love to the world. Yet before their eyes, Jesus suddenly cooperates in his own breaking, piercing and demise. The young male will always find the mature discipleship implied in the paschal cycle inherently forbidding, based as it is on the limits of dying to self. And yet, beyond these limits lies a horizon of unparalleled hope: renewed life, empowerment and even Christ's second coming.

The disciples need to graduate from martial, competitive values (seen in the shadow moment of their quarrel about who is more spiritually eminent and destined to sit next to Jesus in heaven) to more mature ones of greater depth and subtlety. The poet David Whyte describes such a moment in a young man's life in recounting the story of his arrival as a youthful Himalayan trekker at a swinging bridge suspended over a mountain gorge.[27] At this moment, Whyte's powers of masculine prowess deserted him. He sank down, paralysed, terrified at the prospect of the swaying crossing. Suddenly a wizened old woman appeared behind him, as if from nowhere, and nimbly crossed the bridge. Whyte describes her as a kind of angel, inviting him into an appreciation of subtler qualities when his roaring boy ones had failed him. So too Christ's disciples will undergo an intensive process of initiation and growth after Gethsemane. Only then will they become fit for the challenges of the post-Pentecost period. Until that point, they will largely be subject to enforced passivity, spiritually squeezed into protracted inner work and reframed understanding of Christ's mission. Qualities other than male wilfulness will need to emerge in their psyches. They will engage in little decisive action and be cloistered from the public stage. Although they have failed their Gethsemane test, in God's grace they will grow. No past failure is final in God's economy. Our spiritual growth often follows a call denied, botched or wantonly failed.

Nevertheless, the disciples' formation process will be lengthy. They will know forty days of wandering between Jesus' resurrection and his ascension. Forty days is a prototypical biblical passage, of course. Spiritually, it represents a period that always feels far, far longer than any human being would like. The ego covets control but a forty-day passage involves necessary shriving and mortification. We are forced from the outer stage into the inner world. Matters of deep alchemy are taking place within us, primarily surrender to death of self. This is how spiritual transformation begins in human beings. As Terry Eagleton writes: 'The New Testament is a brutal destroyer of human illusions. If you follow Jesus and don't end up dead, it appears you have some explaining to do.'[28]

'I know that beyond any mere ordering of one's affairs, preparing for death means excavating the bedrock of one's relations with other people, teaching oneself to let go.'
Marie de Hennezel[1]

'Beware of refusing to go to the funeral of your own independence. The natural life is not spiritual, and it can only be made spiritual by sacrifice. If we do not resolutely sacrifice the natural, the supernatural can never become natural in us.'
Oswald Chambers[2]

'I tell you the truth, unless a grain of wheat falls to the ground and dies, it remains only a single seed. But if it dies, it produces many seeds.'
John 12:24

3

Crushed

Having surrendered to God's sovereign will, Jesus leaves Gethsemane able to make a pure offering of himself. This is what any of us can achieve in our lives when we too say, 'Your will be done.' Released from potential resentment or religious duty, we can allow the oil of our love to flow as unadulterated gift. The gritty realism of Scripture, however, is that Jesus alone models this way at this point in the gospel narratives. Aside from John protectively accompanying Jesus' mother to the cross and Peter wantonly denying his master, the other disciples are conspicuously absent. Barring a possible cursory reference in Luke 23:49, they have fled the stage. In their relative absence, therefore, Jesus must form the bright sun to which they offer only shadow. Having chosen to give himself freely, Jesus now shows us how to die before we die – to pick up our cross daily with the same grace with which he travels to Calvary.

Pursuing the metaphor of the oil press, we have considered Jesus' 'crushing' in Gethsemane. It might, though, be more accurate to talk of his 'pressing' there, squeezed to yield the oil of healing and salvation for others. His absolute 'crushing' comes in his journey to Calvary and his crucifixion. The cross itself is a mystery with polyvalent meanings. We will examine it primarily here as an invitation into deeper discipleship. However, we must not miss its foundational implications for our salvation. Fifty years ago, A. W. Tozer powerfully reminded his generation of its astringent spiritual power. Condemning 'the new cross' often preached by a liberal church as a friendly sop to the culture, he underscored the savagely terminal nature of 'the old cross', refusing to shy from its horror or dilute its message.[3] For Tozer, the bitter taste of the cross testified to the evil of our sin whose binding power can only be broken through Jesus' death. Following Tozer, when we meditate on Jesus crucified, we more fully understand the living death that we suffer as a result of our sin. We see our spiritual corruption directly imaged. One intended place to which this then takes us is 'metanoia' (a 'turning round' in our mind and heart). Personally, the most decisive transformation that I've ever known followed immediately on my deepest experience of repentance, as tears and hatred for a long-tolerated sin shook my body in waves. By contrast, when I feebly mouth 'Sorry' to God for a sin, having undergone no real 'turning round', my confession lacks depth and transformation is negligible. We do well to remember the words of the hymn 'Come down, O Love divine', which speak of 'true lowliness of heart' that 'o'er its own shortcomings weeps with loathing'.

For the remainder of this chapter we will meditate on the beauty with which Christ bears his passion. Let us not, though, neglect to contemplate the vileness of what he suffers. The cross represents both Christ's beauty and our spiritual darkness, borne by him for us. Our theology must encompass both elements for our fullest growth in discipleship.

We turn now to the cross as an invitation into discipleship, mirroring Jesus' call to pick up our cross daily and follow him. The key paradox of Gethsemane and the cross, vigorously resisted by the disciples until later, is that spiritual growth begins in descent and times of darkness. Again and again Scripture records that new life comes after time spent in a prison cell (Joseph), the belly of a whale (Jonah) or a tomb (Jesus). Descent, though, has always been anathema to the youthful psyche, including, in our own age, Generation Y (those born from the late 1970s to mid-1990s). Professor Paul Harvey, a Gen Y expert, describes this generation as having 'unrealistic expectations and a strong resistance towards accepting negative feedback'.[4] To the person holding 'an inflated view of oneself', the cross will always appear foolishness. It is, however, spiritually essential. If God is most fully revealed in the person of the crucified Christ, it is likely that we will experience God's glory most in our own seasons of darkness.

The deepest insight that the cross offers us of the divine nature, one in which we are first created and then restored as new creations, concerns the profound humility of God. Philippians 2:5–8 famously pictures this in the progressive descent of Christ from the Godhead to incarnate human being to one voluntarily pierced and nailed to the cross. The movement is clear. God's heart always flows to the lowest place, the place of greatest depression and need. Jesus allows himself to be broken open for us. He becomes the man who voluntarily falls to earth, dies for our sake as scapegoat beyond the city walls. As the Apostles' Creed details, he then descends to those souls entombed in hell. In his humility lies a key insight of the cross for our discipleship. Having surrendered in Gethsemane to our call, we must now pass through the waters of death. We equip ourselves to do so by imitating the humility of Christ.

How do we go to the cross humbly? It begins with letting go of our old identity. This may have served us royally in the past. However, it has now become spiritually constraining. If the coordinates of our identity are immovable ('this is how I am'), if we are fiercely defended as people, little change will be possible. For all that evangelicals talk about dying to self, our spirituality to map this process is often impoverished. Ignatian spirituality, by contrast, describes different stages of growth in humility with great acuity. There is the humility of our initial conversion, as we surrender our autonomy to follow Christ; the humility of initial discipleship as we seek not only to follow but to become like Christ, allowing him to grow in us; and the humility of mature discipleship where we choose to identify with Christ's sufferings, his experiences of rejection, humiliation and pain. We are given the imaginative, prayerful and contemplative tools to identify with Jesus' suffering as a daily practice and this practice becomes the ground of our soul's growth.

Nevertheless, the Gethsemane narratives reveal that the path of sacrificial, downward mobility is challenging even for Jesus. In John 21:18, the risen Jesus may recall his own Calvary in describing the path that Peter will need to take to the cross:

> I tell you the truth, when you were younger you dressed yourself and went where you wanted; but when you are old you will stretch out your hands, and someone else will dress you and lead you where you do not want to go.

Peter's tethering directly parallels Jesus being 'bound' by soldiers in Gethsemane (John 18:12) and being led to his trial and death. A rope hauls both God and Peter to the cross. Jesus briefly recoils from this tethering in Gethsemane. Yet it is precisely the one who has been bound in whom the fullest expression of divinity will be revealed:

> It is not through the teaching of Jesus nor through His mighty works that the deepest dimension of the divine glory is disclosed in Jesus and that men are overwhelmed by the divine presence: it is through the fact that, of His own will, He places Himself in men's hands and becomes exposed to whatever they will.[5]

Ropes bind and lead many people in our society into situations that they would prefer to avoid. One thinks of the elderly, ill and severely handicapped. It is in these humbled people that we so often find unmistakable signs of God's grace. So Jesus' deepest nature, too, is revealed in his vulnerability. Jesus on the cross becomes the most fulfilled expression of the character of God. Defended as people, we eschew vulnerability. We seek to remain captains of our destiny, in control. But Christ's passion declares that it is through vulnerability that richest life emerges. This is not a broken vulnerability but a robust one where we say 'Yes' to whatever comes. This is why too we can find insights for our discipleship of daily dying in the example of people approaching personal death. Our small deaths of faithful discipleship are ultimately contained in our larger journey to this ultimate threshold, our dissolution in death.

Marie de Hennezel, an expert in palliative care, incisively describes the experience of hospice patients dying well. In her writings, we can observe three dimensions to a person's meaningful progression to death. Each of these aspects, involving 'the culmination of the shaping of a human being', occurs on the interior and subtle plane of human relations.[6] The first shaping involves a setting right of one's personal relationships. Jesus models this at the Last Supper but we also see it in his forgiving interactions with others on his way to his death. The second shaping involves a person shifting from being a passive victim of their dying to becoming a protagonist of their dying. This we observe as Jesus passes from resisting Gethsemane's cup of suffering to expressing mature submission to his Father's will. The third shaping comprises the dying person reviewing the narrative of his or her life and finding coherence, distinction and purpose in it. It seems to be in the shaping of one's life within a meaningful narrative that the dying person finds peace.

This last point is rather different in Jesus' case. In John's Gospel, from Jesus' first encounter with the disciples, he points to the link between his future suffering and God's glory. At the wedding at Cana, he multiplies wine, just as his own blood will be poured out later. How his disciples contrast with him, failing to understand his every reference to future suffering. Until the two followers on the Emmaus road see his life reinterpreted through Old Testament Scripture, they believe that they have only witnessed a meaningless death. Without true understanding, their discipleship is incomplete. This is why Jesus underlines to them, 'Did not the Christ have to suffer these things and then enter his glory?' (Luke 24:26). His glory is realized not in spite of suffering but through it. He understands the shape of his life. Momentarily setting aside a larger perspective of divinity, de Hennezel's insights demonstrate psychological reasons alone why Jesus is able to bear his dying with grace. He ends his relationships well, becomes the protagonist of his own dying, and agrees to his life's final chapter. Let us now look in more detail at his distinctive fulfilment in dying.

Jesus' first sign of maturity in this phase is in being wholly and completely himself. When the authorities in Gethsemane demand that 'Jesus of Nazareth' identify himself, he replies,

'I am he' (John 18:5). This 'I am' (*ego eimi*) recalls God's self-identification to Moses in Exodus 3:14. As a result of this divine self-naming in Gethsemane, the officials and soldiers recoil and fall to the ground (John 18:6). There is a dramatic shift in the spiritual dynamic of the scene. Jesus' 'I am' illuminates his essential nature in this moment and every succeeding one. We instinctively sense his integrity. We know that he supremely embodies this quality. Yet it is more difficult to pinpoint in what this integrity consists. We can understand it best by its counterpoint in Peter's denial. Sometimes a negative pole helpfully reveals its positive.

Theologians note that Peter's reply to his questioners about whether he is a disciple of Jesus – 'I am not' (John 18:17) – reverses Jesus' 'I am'. Peter's answer by the brazier exposes his hollow identity. Theologians also observe that when he curses, 'I don't know the man' (Matthew 26:74), he could be denying affiliation to Jesus or cursing himself. In one sense, it is himself that he doesn't know. Peter is personally lost. How does this apply to our lives? Have you ever found yourself becoming uncharacteristically angry or uttering a cruel put-down? Perhaps you've later reported to another person, 'I don't know what happened; I wasn't myself.' Only you were. That is the horror. We had been confident of our integrity but now that reflection in the mirror has shattered. We do not hold together in the way that we had thought. Something shameful has irrupted from backstage. A previously unacknowledged part of our character has burst on to the stage of our public life.

Why does this inconvenient truth matter? In a moment, Peter will leave his accusers and weep bitterly outside. His inner coward has only surfaced for a moment. Why can't he repent and move on? For the same reason that none of us can when caught in such a crisis. Ultimately, when Peter is challenged, he implicitly says this: 'Everything I have witnessed for the last three years – the miracle of a banquet appearing from a humble lunch; water multiplying into wine sufficient to resource several wedding banquets; a decomposing corpse walking out of a tomb as a resuscitated friend – is nothing. More, the personal journey of maturation and growth on which I have travelled – is nothing. More than these, the person in whom I have invested my whole life, who knows me better than I know myself, and in whose presence I feel fully alive – is nothing.' No wonder that Peter now experiences emotional and spiritual collapse. I suspect this collapse might have been absolute, resulting in a suicide similar to Judas', were it not for prayers that Jesus had prayed earlier. For in Luke 22:31–32, Jesus tells Peter, 'Simon, Simon, Satan has asked to sift you as wheat. But I have prayed for you, Simon, that your faith may not fail. And when you have turned back, strengthen your brothers.' Jesus' prayers save Peter. Peter, like us, cannot ever save himself.

It is at Calvary that a person embraces or rejects personhood. Peter fails this test. He remains in a prison of his making until his conversation weeks later with Jesus on the beach. Yet we must not magnify our outrage at Peter's denial and miss our own transgression. One of the most helpful ways that we might avoid this comes in a formulation of the American educator and activist, Parker Palmer. He describes how social expectations and pressures (evident in Peter's confrontation by the brazier) can force us to live in hiding from our authentic selfhood. We then live enslaved while inhabiting private momentary fantasies of a world set right. Conversely, people who care for their authentic selfhood make a different decision. In Palmer's words:

> They decide to live 'divided no more'. They decide no longer to act on the outside in a way that contradicts some truth about

> themselves that they hold deeply on the inside. They decide to claim authentic selfhood and act it out – and their decisions ripple out to transform the society in which they live, serving the selfhood of millions of others.[7]

Palmer calls this the 'Rosa Parks decision', citing the example of the African American seamstress who one December day in 1955 refused to give up her bus seat to a white person.[8] He describes how she found that courage by reframing her idea of punishment, seeing it now not in a prison sentence that she might serve but in the existential diminishment that she would know if she continued to obey unjust white law. Parks chose to live 'divided no more'. Where we often live in dissociation in our lives, accepting injustice perpetuated against us while only inwardly protesting or nursing fantasies of resistance, Parks moved into a place of integrity. She chose to act according to the imperatives of her moral and spiritual beliefs. This moment not only catalysed her personal transformation, it acted as the tipping point for countless other dramas of societal change in black–white relations in America. So it is on a far larger, cosmic canvas when Jesus acts with integrity and accepts his walk to the cross. Unlike Peter who disappears into the shadows, Jesus becomes fully visible and present. He says little, does little, is principally done to, but his passion wins us salvation, transforms lives and initiates cosmic redemption.

Peter, in denying Christ, becomes a divided person. Jesus, by drinking his cup, embraces mature personhood. His dying to self yields fullness of life. This, of course, Peter was also ultimately to experience. In Caravaggio's 1601 painting of his death, three executioners haul up Peter nailed upside down on a cross.[9] Peter's face now exudes calm acceptance. His executioners' faces, by contrast, are masked in shadow. There could be no more expressive illustration of their lack of personhood, in contrast to Peter's radiant integrity.

This brings us to a second example of Jesus' fulfilment in his passion. Jesus' bodily breaking demonstrates the inextricability of pain and growth. It also raises the question of how we as his disciples are to go to our own graves (whether final or daily) with grace. It is not enough to agree to go there if we are consumed by bitterness or recrimination. That is not a motif of spiritual maturation. Instead, one of Jesus' key active deeds during his passion is to extend forgiveness to the criminal at his side and the executioners who taunt him. How are we to follow him in extending such grace?

The 2015 terrorist attacks in Paris left 130 people dead. One remarkable reaction to this mayhem was that of Antoine Leiris, a young man whose wife, Hélène, died. On his Facebook page after the attack, he issued a poignant tribute, pledging not to let his 17-month-old son grow up in fear of ISIS. To his wife's killers he wrote:

> I will not give you the satisfaction of hating you. You want it, but to respond to hatred with anger would be to give in to the same ignorance that made you what you are. You would like me to be scared, for me to look at my fellow citizens with a suspicious eye, for me to sacrifice my liberty for my security. You have lost.[10]

Leiris understands that hatred would bind him to his wife's killers, locking him into fear and distrust. He knows that unforgiveness will become a prison. The release of hatred that we feel is finally little compensation for the power that we yield to our abusers. It is, though, some way from Leiris's position to being able to extend forgiveness and even blessing to those who harm us. Jesus doesn't refuse to hate as part of a territorial refusal to surrender his faith in humanity. He

our default habit to die. This is why we need the focus of a higher affection (for the Christian, Jesus) and to pick up our cross daily. All the transformation that comes to Jesus and his disciples in the paschal cycle comes through their reaching new thresholds and giving things up. To make a sacred journey, we always have to make a sacrifice. Something has to be forsaken so that something greater can be gained. This is why Oswald Chambers warns against our refusing to go to the funeral of our own independence. He reminds us that only through sacrifice can the natural in us be made supernatural.

I discovered this in my own case when my embrace of the higher affection of love led me, six months later, to an Alpha course to explore the claims of Christianity and, six months after that, as a new Christian, to the beloved woman whom I would marry. That was one full year later, by which time I had been intentionally celibate for two years. Sacrifice matures us. By contrast, sacred journeys lacking the element of sacrifice do little work in us. Phil Cousineau writes of a female mythology scholar heading a tour through Ireland in the mid-1990s. She led her pilgrims to the Skellig islands off the west coast of Ireland, with their ancient monastic settlements built atop craggy pinnacles of rock. The weather and sea conditions for this visit were unusually propitious. Yet, when the pilgrims returned from the islands, they erupted in anger over minor problems with their accommodation. The scholar observed:

> Ironically, this mythically difficult journey proved to be too easy! So I learned that day when travel is too easy, people often don't appreciate their experience and certainly don't understand the mythological nature of certain kinds of travel.[15]

The paschal journey is not intended to be easy. It demands choice, commitment and sacrifice, and comes at a cost.

Embracing the higher affection of following Jesus, we break habits of the old self and come more into the likeness of him (Philippians 2:5; 1 Corinthians 2:16). We receive his attributes made transferable by his death. The fruits of the Holy Spirit, the expressions of his lovely character, grow in us. It begins, though, with crucifixion. We must die to ourselves. Ultimately, we can measure our maturity by the number of empty tombs that we leave behind us, provided that these deaths yield new life. One of the reasons that the disciples abort their Gethsemanes is that they fail to see Jesus' likely death as leading to life. They understand his death as the death of their hopes instead of what it really is – the foundation of their hopes on a wider level than they have ever known before. When we think that dying to self is fatal, terminal, and that we will never recover, we see only loss. We need to be re-educated. We need to live in the resurrection. Then we can see that there is purpose to our daily dying and a new life beyond death. In this, it is, of course, easier for us than for Peter and the disciples. We are not simply empty-tomb people but third-day people. We have read about the risen Christ and have met him in our own life ourselves.

At the same time, even armed with the wisdom of the paschal cycle, it does seem existentially difficult for us to 'die'. This is why Charlie Cleverly insisted that the message of my ordination was about coming to rest in the sepulchre of the church. The death of my old life had to be absolute. All of it had to go to the grave. So it is when I meet people in my church for pastoral counselling. Sometimes one has to let the person hit rock bottom and know a personal death of their old identity. Sometimes one has to resist pulling the nails out of their crucified flesh and resist seeing them rise before they have fully died. There is a resurrection to come but there is also a Good Friday to endure first, a good one being the bitterest of ones. Death must be final. And then the person must fully live 'the long day's journey of the Saturday'.[16] Only after that will new life come.

'There is one particular day in Western history about which neither historical record nor myth nor Scripture make report. It is a Saturday. And it has become the longest of days . . . Ours is the long day's journey of the Saturday. Between suffering aloneness, unutterable waste on the one hand and the dream of liberation, of rebirth on the other.'
George Steiner[1]

'The process of transformation consists mostly of decay.'
Rebecca Solnit[2]

'I, when I am lifted up from the earth,
will draw all people to myself.'
Jesus in John 12:32 (NIV 2011)

4
Buried

We live in an age of darkness. John Paul II memorably termed it 'the culture of death'.[3] It is not hard to see signs of this darkness, whether in acts of nihilistic violence or the terminal pessimism of much contemporary art. Ever since the Victorian poet Matthew Arnold evoked the 'melancholy, long, withdrawing roar' of 'the sea of Faith' in *Dover Beach*, artists and writers have reiterated a secular position resistant to transcendent hope.[4] For literary critic George Steiner, our culture now lives a haunted Saturday existence, beached between a Friday of pain and suffering and a future Sunday of redemption. Steiner suggests that, whether religious or non-religious, we experience a Saturday absence of God in our frustrated longings and disappointed dreams. Even atheists, he writes, carry a sense of Sunday as 'the day of liberation from inhumanity and servitude'.[5] Our secular culture inhabits a twilight world, 'the long day's journey of the Saturday', having absorbed failure, loss and pain, unable to access Sunday's better world. This is where we left Edward in *On Chesil Beach*, camped out bitterly in the place of his failed relationship. Here the tomb is indeed a dead end. No deeper magic reigns. Edward remains stalled, failing to mature and grow. Years later, he reflects on his life: 'He had drifted through, half asleep, inattentive, unambitious, unserious, childless, comfortable.'[6] Edward's failure should have been temporary. He has clung to it with resentment, though, claiming it as his own. In this he stands as a cultural type of much of our age.

To Christians, Sunday's hope is real, tangible and embodied, witnessed in the person of the risen Christ. It has been said that calling and dying both reveal what, or whom, we love. We are called into vocations that embody our particular loving gift to the world. Marie de Hennezel's dying patients frequently discover, even if late in life, whom and what it is they really love. For the dying atheist, this love is present or retrospective, a love for people known and cherished, and that too is a wonder. For the dying Christian, though, love also anticipates an eternity with a lover who has risen from the tomb: Jesus Christ. Yet in our discipleship we can also learn from the atheist's experience of Holy Saturday. In one sense, it is vital for transformation that we genuinely sit in the ashes of our losses, rather than rushing towards the dawn of any personal resurrection. Holy Saturday invites us to sit with the bitterness of premature losses and feel their sting.

This paschal phase addresses how we sit with suffering and honour this moment. Our model is Jesus. In Gethsemane Jesus allows himself to be bound by rope when he could summon twelve legions of angels to his side. He drinks the cup and thereby frees himself from future bitterness. Nailed to the cross, he refuses the anaesthetic of wine mixed with myrrh, identifying totally with our suffering. He absorbs every hatred hurled at him and radiates back only forgiveness and love. Through this redemptive posture, he will rise to trample death and evil. In his agony, recalled in the wounds he carries in his risen state, he will gather up every suffering from history in himself and God.

As disciples, we too cannot short-circuit the depth process of change. Only through agreeing to darkness' embrace can we genuinely die to what has been. This is dangerous territory. We can get existentially lost in this wilderness. That is why we need rites of passage. A rite's 'liminal space' provides a structured territory in which necessary decomposition and grieving can occur. It acts as an 'in-between' place, in which we leave behind what we have known, and we are carried, protected, until future context emerges. Rites of passage hold us between an evocation of what has been and what is to come, condensing our trust. Our innate human desire is to collapse the tension of this life season, retreating into the past or fast-forwarding into the future. By contrast, when Joseph in his prison trusts in God, even that place of darkness yields treasure. Joseph's years there shape his character and deepen his faith.

We can measure our personal response to dying, death and burial as part of personal change through four sets of figures in the passion narrative. The first set is the disciples, conspicuously absent at the cross. We can only conjecture about their psychological and spiritual state. They must be shattered, having experienced the death of their dreams. Whereas the beloved disciple John chooses to stand under the cross, compassionately sharing in his master's suffering, the other disciples hide. Their fear overshadows their love for Jesus. Metaphorically, they may already be, like the two followers on the road to Emmaus, 'leaving Jerusalem'. These are young men who have been energized by messianic prospects of martial victory. Now their reaction to loss is shock. They stand for every part of us that demands a strong Jesus of our choosing and that resists a Jesus who is weak and the voice of love. Like many men, they have assayed the 'heroic' role and failed. Vulnerable and broken, they skulk in the shadows.

For the group of women at the foot of the cross, our second set of figures, it is different. The feminine spirit does not deal in heroic absolutes. Mary's cohort remains faithful and grieving, perhaps possessed of some deeper intuition. They are companioning presences to Jesus. They refuse to turn away from his agony. De Hennezel, describing her work with hospice patients, talks of the heartfelt work of accompanying a dying person. Discussing the need for empathetic involvement as well as reasonable professional limits, she offers this telling observation about her medical staff:

> I have often seen for myself how the medical personnel who protect themselves the most are also those who complain the most of being exhausted. Those who give themselves, however, also recharge themselves at the same time . . . Love, far from being a reservoir that begins to drain with use, refills the more it overflows.[7]

The women beneath the cross possess themselves completely. Unlike the disciples, they remain present, visible, dignified in grief. These grieving women recall the Chilean mothers of 'the disappeared' who regularly paraded in Santiago's main square during General Pinochet's regime. Dressed in black, these women would silently process, bearing photographs of their loved ones who had 'vanished' under Pinochet's ghastly rule. Their very presence was a protest. In the same way, Mary and her group implicitly challenge the rulers, authorities and powers of this dark world who have nailed the sinless Jesus to the tree. They represent the part of us that remains present to suffering, pondering, in the place of fire.

It is worth considering further the contrast between the male disciples and this female group. Aside from John, the beloved disciple who draws close to his master, we see here a stark gender divide. The male psyche, strong as long as it can embrace absolutes, often fares less well in holding anxiety and living with ambiguity. The female psyche dwells more easily on thresholds, accepting liminality, faithful to the complex truth of what it experiences. The women don't flee, don't seek to explain, linger, despite the fact that they too face the death of their dreams about Jesus. The loss of their personal dreams never takes precedence over their human affinity for the one whom they have lost. Their love triumphs over fear or personal shock. In their hierarchy of values, they prioritize people above agendas. The disciples come across as scattered and divided individuals with no constellating person behind whom to group. The women unite behind Mary, drawn together by her spirit of motherhood. In this, they offer a lesson in discipleship that does not take flight from ambivalence or vulnerability.

Our third figure is the beloved disciple, John. He dwells close to the cross, in contrast to his fellow disciples. At the Last Supper, he rested his head on Jesus' breast. He abided in Jesus, sensing his anguish, offering love, comfort and trust. Pressing into intimacy with Jesus, he shared and bore the burdens of Jesus' heart. He perfectly accepted the Jesus who washed feet and who will endure betrayal and give up his life for his friends. Now, standing directly beneath the cross (for Jesus' voice would have been barely audible through the asphyxiating effects of crucifixion), John suffers with Jesus. He allows himself to be 'crucified with Christ' (Galatians 2:20). The John in us is the part that does not try to conform Jesus to our own imagination or ideology but allows ourselves to be shaped to the truth of who he is. John, comforting Jesus' mother, is a type of the undefended person who hazards heartbreak and is drawn deeper into a wider family of love. Peter has not yet learned to be loved by Jesus. He wants an all-conquering Messiah, not a vulnerable master who washes his feet. John, the beloved, receives Jesus as he is. We may gravitate more towards one or other tendency, the impulsive activist or the contemplative mystic, or we may know their contradictory traits warring within us. Both are vital, though, for God's economy and, as we shall see, for the future church. If we have much of Peter in us, we will need to give up a false Jesus of our making and draw closer to the suffering servant. If we have much of John in us, we will be acquainted with sorrow but will need to integrate the energy and resilience of the disciple known as the Rock (Matthew 16:18).

The disciples hide; the women and John remain present. From our third set of figures, the death of Jesus elicits a different response. Joseph of Arimathea and Nicodemus do not take flight or openly grieve for Jesus beneath the cross. Rather, in its aftermath, they arrange his burial, newly self-identifying as his disciples. Jesus' death acts as their moment of call. So we too at defining moments of our lives embrace the new and emerge from obscurity into presence and visibility. Previously concealed commitment now shows itself. We become more of the people that God has made us to be. This will often be in contrast to what our culture would like of us. Any society seeks to render certain of its citizens invisible. The narrator of *Invisible Man*, a 1952 American novel by Ralph Ellison, is an unnamed African American man living in a segregated culture:

> I was pulled this way and that for longer than I can remember. And my problem was that I always tried to go in everyone's way but my own. I have also been called one thing and then another while no one really wished to hear what I called myself. So after

> years of trying to adopt the opinions of others I finally rebelled. I am an invisible man.[8]

Today's Western secular society politely pressurizes Christians to remain invisible (albeit our position remains very different from that of black Americans in 1950s America). However, God's call is for us to be fully visible, a light on a hill. In their startling response to Jesus' death, Joseph and Nicodemus, formerly covert disciples, reject complicity with the culture and become protagonists on the public stage. It is an astonishing move for two members of the Sanhedrin, the ruling body which only twenty-four hours before found Jesus guilty of blasphemy.

Luke describes Joseph as 'a good and upright man, who had not consented to their [the Council's] decision and action' (Luke 23:50–51). A wealthy, prominent figure, he has been a disciple of Jesus 'but secretly because he feared the Jews' (John 19:38). Nicodemus, a doctrinally orthodox Pharisee and their pre-eminent teacher, has learned from Jesus that law and good works can't save him. He must be born again by the Spirit. He will only accept this lesson, though, under cover of darkness. In short, we see two men on whom Jesus has had an impact but who, until now, were constrained by public position and fear of others' opinions. John has talked earlier in his Gospel of men who 'would not confess their faith for fear they would be put out of the synagogue; for they loved praise from men more than praise from God' (John 12:42–43). Following Jesus' death, however, Joseph 'went boldly to Pilate and asked for Jesus' body' (Mark 15:43). Nicodemus aids him in the burial. Both men now commit to Jesus at the very moment that Peter, his hitherto committed follower, denies him. It is an astonishing turnaround. What can possibly explain this earthquake in their lives?

Joseph and Nicodemus have surely witnessed the crucifixion, along with the chief priests and other teachers of the law (Mark 15:31–32). As they gaze up at Jesus' crucified body, the Holy Spirit speaks to them of Jesus' beauty and convicts them of their own darkness. As John Stott notes, 'Before we can begin to see the cross as something done *for* us . . . we have to see it as something done *by* us.'[9] Joseph intuits that Jesus has given himself as a fragrant offering for his bride. Now Joseph must honour the bridegroom. Peter Kreeft writes: 'We sinned for no reason but an incomprehensible lack of love, and He saved us for no reason but an incomprehensible excess of love.'[10] Joseph and Nicodemus reciprocate Jesus' marvellous affection by risking their futures, wrapping his body in fragrant spices and publicly honouring him in death.

How do Joseph and Nicodemus speak into our discipleship? While the disciples take flight from Golgotha, refusing conversation with an emerging reality that they are unready to face, and the women lament at Golgotha, tethered in shock to the present moment, Joseph and Nicodemus signify the part of us that is always moving ahead, crossing boundaries and reaching for a new horizon. This part of our imagination and psyche moves ahead, even in darkness, not grasping after an over-idealized future but opening to a more generous conversation. Through awakening to the larger context beyond their lives, these two men pioneer a deeply creative act in the hour of greatest darkness. At the bleakest moment in the paschal cycle, they offer their gift, become visible and do something beautiful for God. In Parker Palmer's terms, they come to live divided no more. In so doing, they unwittingly fulfil Old Testament prophecy about the circumstances of Jesus' burial (Isaiah 53:9). They unlock divine destiny and become a prophetic sign of God's unfolding purposes.

It is time to consider what it looks like in a person's life when that person agrees to enter the tomb, with Christ, as part of the process of change. One familiar metaphor given for this process is the transition from caterpillar to chrysalis to butterfly. This metaphor, like much else to do with change in the Christian life, is often represented in simplistic terms. Rebecca Solnit, who has studied this biological process first-hand, offers a more sober perspective. In place of a language of thresholds as fluid, beautiful and graceful (as in the phrase 'death-rebirth'), Solnit emphasizes the process's jolting convulsions. Consider her description of embryonic butterflies struggling free from their chrysalises:

> They came out with their wings packed down like furled parachutes, like crumpled letters . . . Some did not get quite free, and their wings never fully straightened. One butterfly sat still with an orange wing curled into the chrysalis. One seemed permanently stuck halfway out, its yellow-and-black wings like buds that would not flower. One flailed frantically, trying to drag itself out by crawling onto adjacent unopened chrysalises until they too began to thrash, a contagious panic. That one finally dropped free, though it may have been too late for its wings to straighten. The process of transformation consists mainly of decay and then of this crisis when emergence from what came before must be total and abrupt.[11]

In the change process, we may feel trapped in a corner, in danger of disappearance. We can shudder with anxiety and feel panic, fearful that emergence will not come. When it does, it frequently arrives as a crisis. There are convulsions and a necessary fighting for life. Moreover, in the early stages of emergence, we may look very little like the person we had hoped to be. Of course, not all changes in a caterpillar's life are so dramatic. Frequently, as it grows, it splits its skin in successive moults. Yet its most fundamental metamorphosis is more of an abrupt jolt than a graceful unfolding. So it can be with us in decisive moments of discipleship growth.

If you are currently caught in this 'buried' phase and, like Solnit's butterfly, frantically flailing, be reassured. This is an entirely normal aspect of the change process. It is just that no-one has ever articulated to you its biological and anthropological realities. You may feel locked in a tight corner. However, your death will not be terminal. You are actually on a threshold. You will find your strength. You will push through.

In summary, the biological transformation of a caterpillar underlines six foundational truths about spiritual change:

1. Only through a radical moulting can a higher form of life emerge.
2. Evolution to the next phase of life demands a fundamental reorganization of self.
3. Struggle and even crisis are intrinsic to the process of transformation.
4. Any new form of life is fragile, provisional and a fledgling requiring nurture.
5. All the constituent elements for new life are biologically, and spiritually, present.
6. You can trust in the process. Surrender. Be complicit. Reach for new life.

Let me ground such change in three contemporary case histories. The first involves my own. Earlier I described embracing the higher affection of 'love' during a tumultuous phase of my life. At the same time, aged forty, I hit a vocational crisis. I experienced what existential psychologist James Bugental would term 'the nevers' of mid-life: 'I guess that I'm never going to be the head of the firm . . . never going to have children of my own . . . never going to be a great writer . . . never going to be rich . . . never going to be famous.'[12] My own insight was that I would never both be the fabulously successful theatre director of my dreams and establish solid ground to marry and have children. My theatre vocation was too demanding and financially precarious. Along with embracing celibacy at this time in a desire to rediscover the meaning of love, I therefore chose to end my twenty-year theatre career. I had no plan. I just knew that I had to lower the theatre director in me into the grave. The following months were hard. I wept every day. I felt lost. I read every book I could lay my hands on about career change. Finally, a new dream surfaced in my mind. It seemed absurd but it captivated my imagination. I fantasized about it, mused on it, talked it over with others. What was my projected career? To become a funeral director, offering a contemporary rite of passage for our culture.

How amusing, in retrospect. Of course, I now see this dream as the last gasp of my pre-Christian struggle to answer one of life's biggest questions: what happens at death and how do we honour the one who has gone? More than this, I see that I mistook a metaphor (managing a death) for a reality (a career). I was in the 'buried' phase of the paschal drama and needed to die to theatre directing. It was never about my becoming a funeral director, even though today as an Anglican priest I lead funeral services. What was going on was that my psyche was helpfully trying to stage-manage the death of my existing career identity. Meditating on being a funeral director became an unwitting way of bidding theatre directing goodbye. After a month or two of entertaining this idea, something in me shifted. At some level, I realized that I could drop what had only been a metaphor for an inner process. I abandoned this path for a much more fruitful opportunity in a documentary company where I could exercise transferable skills.

Some individuals go further in their self-burial and decomposition in order to trigger spiritual breakthrough and transformation. The twentieth-century German artist Joseph Beuys (1921–86) was one such person. Although not avowedly a Christian, Beuys used Christian motifs throughout his artistic work. Before his breakthrough as an international artist, he struggled. At the age of thirty-three, he entered his most testing years. Physically exhausted as a result of multiple war wounds, his morale plummeted over his persistent failure to succeed as an artist. Then at Christmas 1954 his younger fiancée returned to him her engagement ring. Severe depression engulfed Beuys and he entered a dark wood. He wandered, sought treatment in psychiatric clinics and locked himself away for weeks in a friend's vacant flat:

> He kept saying that he wanted to disappear and needed nothing more than a backpack. During this phase Beuys had a carpenter from Kleve make himself a wooden crate, which he insisted on having smoothly planed and finished. Then he smeared tar all over this beautifully finished crate, inside and out, and took it to his studio in Heerdt. His idea, as he later recalled, was that the crate was a black, empty, isolated space, in which investigations could take place and new experiences could occur. He felt compelled to sit inside it, to not be anymore, to simply stop living . . . Utterly worn out, Beuys felt estranged from humanity; he lost even more weight, lapsed into mental inertia, and without energy, became a wreck in every sense. This went on for two years or so. Then something happened that triggered a turn of events.[13]

That 'something' involved Beuys going to stay on the farm of two friends, brothers, whose mother had been recently widowed. Working on the land, doing his daily duty and influenced by the solid, practical psychology of the farming family, Beuys began to recover. Drawn out of isolation and into family, physically toiling in nature, he slowly entered a new phase of health and remarkable artistic activity. Going on to become Germany's most celebrated contemporary artist, Beuys never looked back.

Now, I don't want to romanticize Beuys' two years of darkness from 1956 to 1957. Much of it suggests considerable mental ill health. This kind of willed deterioration in a person can offend us. Nevertheless, at a deep level, I believe that, caught in a long process of decomposition, Beuys sought to mine this darkness. Somewhere inside him, he trusted it as a doorway to spiritual and creative regeneration. Ignored by the art world, rejected by his fiancée, thrown back on himself, he realized that he had exhausted his resources. He knew that he needed to break out and move forward into new territory. He just didn't know how to reach that place. His primary goal therefore became to 'leave home', to end his existing conversation with the world, and to wander unencumbered, carrying only a 'backpack'. He created a jet-black tomb-like, womb-like space to act as a precipitating threshold. He understood that, rather than needing 'a way out' of his situation, he needed 'a way in'. He sought to amplify and make more real his threshold experience. As in Solnit's account, he both experienced decomposition and made efforts to catalyse change. Readers may differ in opinions of whether his method was wise but I would suggest that, for all its apparent chaos, itwas threshold inner work of a high order. Sometimes a person harbours a deep hunger for spiritual (and, in this case, creative) emergence. However, a mighty process of breakdown and reorganization of body, mind and spirit must take place before that hunger can be fulfilled.

In later life Beuys explicitly described his mental illness and depression in terms of a process of purification:

> Wartime events no doubt played a part in that crisis, but present events did too, because basically something had to die out. I think it was one of the most essential phases for me; I totally reorganized myself, even constitutionally. I had spent too long just dragging my body around. Initially it was a general state of exhaustion that quickly transformed into a true process of renewal. Things inside me had to change completely, there had to be a metamorphosis, physically as well. Illnesses are nearly always mental crises in one's life, in which old experiences and thought processes are rejected or recast as entirely positive changes . . .
>
> Sure, many people never go through this process of reorganization, but when you get through it a lot of things that were previously unclear or only vaguely outlined take on a completely viable new direction. This sort of crisis is a sign of either a lack of direction or of too many directions being taken at once. It is an unmistakable call to rectify things and to come to new solutions in specific directions. From then on, I began to work systematically, according to definite principles.[14]

Beuys positions this type of breakdown within the context of a larger calling. Many people will compromise and settle for a lesser life rather than hazard such deterioration. For the Christian, though, dying to self is not an optional prescription but a command of Christ. Dying daily, we may avoid the need for such tectonic shifts. For some, though, spiritual growth does involve this kind of rigorous process. Depending on personality, we may or may not identify with Beuys' existential choices. However, it only takes a cursory reading of his life to appreciate the tremendous personal and social fruit that he subsequently bore as an educator, artist, activist and social thinker.

Our final discipleship portrait is more challenging still. Mother Teresa, the Albanian nun, toiled for decades in the slums of Calcutta, helping the reviled and abandoned in whom she saw Jesus. Since the publication of her letters to spiritual confidantes, a new dimension of her story has emerged. For over four decades, following her prayer in 1951 to share in Christ's sufferings, Mother Teresa experienced profound doubts and a continuing dark night of the soul. In Christian mysticism, God inhabits a light so dazzling that it masks his glory in a dark cloud of unknowing. Mother Teresa spent much of her spiritual life in this cloud, initially coveting it in prayer and then suffering it in a Golgotha of abandonment. Yet dwelling in this long day's night she remained obedient to her calling to help the poor. She trusted in God in her darkness. In her letters, at times, she even gives thanks for its treasures. Thus, she writes: 'I have come to love the darkness. For I believe now that it is a part, a very, very small part of Jesus' darkness and pain on earth.'[15] She continues, speaking of her deep joy 'that Jesus can't go anymore through the agony – but that He wants to go through it in me'.[16]

Mother Teresa devoutly indwelt this spiritual phase of the paschal mystery. She embraced the darkest part of Christ's earthly life, dying and death. She buried herself in its pitch night. In the midst of this, she ministered beautifully for God, exemplifying a type of contemporary sainthood. Hers may be the narrowest of gates passed through but we can marvel at her example and draw courage from it for our times of trials. Above all, she embodied obedience to God's call in spite of her Father's silence, something that C. S. Lewis regards as the highest form of spiritual commitment. In *The Screwtape Letters*, the demon Screwtape confides to his nephew, Wormwood:

> Our cause is never more in danger than when a human, no longer desiring, but still intending, to do your Enemy's [God's] will, looks round upon a universe from which every trace of him seems to have vanished, and asks why he has been forsaken, and still obeys.[17]

Mother Teresa in her letters did indeed ask why she had been forsaken. She doubted God, yet she persisted. She held fast. She obeyed. She identified with Jesus in his crucifixion. By his stripes, men and women in the slums of Calcutta were healed.

The 'buried' phase of discipleship growth has been evident in this chapter's dense images: darkness, Matthew Arnold's retreating sea, the long day's journey of the Saturday, the tomb. This is the landscape in which we are called to die. Growth comes when we seek this darkness' buried treasure. We observe this in the example of Nicodemus and Joseph of Arimathea. Burial does not mean the end of hope. When we mine darkness, act as a protesting presence to evil, honour the fragrance of Christ and become visible in his defence, we discover that we can be spiritually creative even in the blackest night. We may temporarily feel abandoned by God, as Christ did when he uttered his great cry of agony on the cross. God, though, waits for us beyond our feelings of abandonment. Life may seem fatally to pen us in, but we move in anticipation towards a larger horizon. We wait in faith. We become prophets of a better future. Now, though, it is time to move on from this time of deepest darkness and Holy Saturday, from what Shakespeare calls 'the dark backward and abysm of time'.[18] For the tomb is ultimately only a chrysalis and the third day is coming. The stone will be rolled away. Reshaped and resurrected, we will walk forth from the tomb.

'Today, in terms of feeling, we live in that time between Good Friday and Easter Sunday. We are trudging along the road to Emmaus. Like the two disciples, we live with crucified dreams. Aesthetically, romantically, ethically, and religiously, we are surrounded by despair and its child, cynicism.'
Ronald Rolheiser[1]

'Lost really has two disparate meanings. Losing things is about the familiar falling away, getting lost is about the unfamiliar appearing . . . Either way, there is a loss of control.'
Rebecca Solnit[2]

'Though the doors were locked, Jesus came and stood among them and said, "Peace be with you!" Then he said to Thomas, "Put your finger here; see my hands. Reach out your hand and put it into my side. Stop doubting and believe." Thomas said to him, "My Lord and my God!" Then Jesus told him, "Because you have seen me, you have believed; blessed are those who have not seen and yet have believed."'
John 20:26–29

5

Breathed on

When anxious friends broke into the locked flat where Joseph Beuys was staying and found him in a dark room, legs swollen with oedema, the artist later commented: 'I believe that those who found me observed that they could literally have pulled the flesh from my bone. That was how far gone from life I was.'[3] Beuys' recovery amounted to revivification. Although not dead, he returned to life, like Lazarus. Astonishing though his healing was, it is still far removed from what happens to Jesus: the glory of resurrection. This is a miracle without comparison in the history of the world. I still remember well how foundational coming to believe in the historical reality of Christ's resurrection was to my conversion. Already convinced of the authenticity of his life and death, I now became fully persuaded by the evidence of the gospel narratives, the disciples' transformation, and my own experience of meeting the risen Jesus in prayer. Every Christian will be familiar with the catalytic difference that the truth of Jesus' resurrection makes for our personal identity and destiny in this life and the next. Romans 6 speaks of how, having been buried with Christ through baptism into death, 'we too may live a new life' through his rising and 'will certainly also be united with him in his resurrection' (vv. 4–5). However, vital though this is to grasp doctrinally for our formation, it is not where the Gospel accounts of the resurrection begin.

These omit to depict Jesus' rising or departing from the tomb. They elide that miracle and mystery. Instead, they focus on encounter, those moments of meeting between the risen Jesus and his followers. C. S. Lewis, reimagining such an encounter in *The Lion, The Witch and The Wardrobe*, describes the risen Aslan appearing to Susan and Lucy. As the girls stand in disbelief and awe, the great lion licks Susan's forehead. She is caught up in his warm breath and the rich smell hanging around his hair. Next Lucy cries, 'Oh, you're real, you're real! Oh, Aslan!', and the girls throw themselves on him, showering him with kisses. Only after this does reflective insight come: '"But what does it all mean?" asked Susan when they were somewhat calmer.'[4]

The Gospel accounts of the risen Jesus begin with the shock of encounter and only gradually proceed to the theological question of 'what it all means'. Acts 1:3 records that Jesus appeared to the disciples 'over a period of forty days and spoke about the kingdom of God'. In the first instance, though, the writers record how the disciples experience the simultaneously startling and incredibly ordinary signs of new life. Their re-education comes later. This chapter is therefore principally concerned with the discipleship question of how we recognize new life in the spiritual: identifying it, welcoming it and cooperating with it fully.

The resurrection is the moment of eternity's sunrise. God's kingdom flowers in our temporal world, pointing prophetically to all that we are to become. Nevertheless, examined dispassionately, the resurrection narratives contain relatively few expressions of unmitigated, sustained joy. John, of course, speaks of the disciples being 'overjoyed' at Jesus' first appearance to them in the locked room (20:20), and Matthew speaks of the women being 'afraid yet filled with joy' as they hurry from their meeting with the angel at the tomb (28:8). The dominant tone, though, in the narratives of Jesus' risen appearances is disorientation. Joy co-mingles with fear, shame, disbelief or confusion. While Paul's epistles enshrine the doctrinal implications of the resurrection, the Gospels testify in a gratifyingly honest way to our human resistance to understanding and embracing the new. How marvellous that we have both, the epistles anchoring the resurrection's doctrinal meaning in God's sovereign plan and the Gospels describing the disciples' very human response to this dead man rising. For even in the revelatory moment when the disciples realize that Jesus has risen, new questions of identity, continuity and purpose erupt. It is as if the brick wall that they had hit at Calvary now melts away. What are they to do in front of a horizon wider than any human being has ever known? It is our profoundly human response to the miracle of risen life that the Gospel writers explore.

We can observe two distinctive, initial elements in the accounts of Jesus' rising. The first is that he still carries his wounds. The Latin root of our word 'vulnerable' is *vulnus*, meaning 'wound', and the risen Jesus appears as the wounded, vulnerable one. For Charles Spurgeon, who has a very healthy theology of Jesus' wounds, the wounds are signs of Christ's suffering love. They are not just temporary identifying marks for the disciples but fundamental to Christ's divine nature; thus the apostle John in his heavenly vision in Revelation sees 'a Lamb looking as if it had been slain' (5:6). We do not have a risen Messiah with an untouched, invulnerable body. He announces, in his very body, that suffering love, rather than martial force, has overcome evil and death. He does not appear in triumphant glory over the temple but carries scars that testify to God's glory. Any mature spirituality must recognize the significance of Jesus' radiant scars for our discipleship. The Gospels are again instructing us that God's transformative power is made manifest in suffering, not in some invulnerable, polished perfection more appropriate to the realm of superheroes. This is good news for any of us aware of our brokenness and need for restoration. As Spurgeon observes of the risen Jesus: 'His wounds are healed wounds – mark – they are not running sores! And so, though we are the wounded parts of Christ, we shall be healed!'[5]

Joseph Beuys understood this theology of the wound. Frequently broken in his body as a result of wartime injuries and illnesses, he became a prophetic artist able to represent in artistic form the hidden wounds of post-war Western society. Convinced of the need for contemporary humanity to get in touch with its brokenness for healing, in 1974–5 he created the artwork *Show Your Wound*.[6] This was an appeal to his audiences to participate in a personal and collective act of transformation. So too the risen Christ appears prophetically, reminding those whom he meets of the wounds and divisions within themselves and their nations, divisions that can be healed only through his reconciling work on the cross. His scars carry us deeper into the paschal paradox: new life comes by way of suffering love.

The second striking feature of Jesus' resurrection appearances is in how they combine both supernatural elements and everyday ordinariness. Jesus walks through walls but also eats, cooks and breaks bread. This paradoxical mixture speaks much about the way in which we experience risen life. If we were looking for a film director to realize these resurrection scenes, we would need to turn to an Andrei Tarkovsky, with his cinematic metaphysics, rather than a Steven Spielberg, with his comforting narrative robustness. In Tarkovsky's 1979 film, *Stalker*, three characters travel through a mysterious mist-shrouded Zone in search of a reported Room in which one's innermost personal desires are granted. Riding through fog on an ancient railway work car, in a state of nervous disorientation, they seem to pass from present to past to present. One critic, writing of the film, says, 'The Zone is a place – a state – of heightened alertness to everything', continuing:

> Landscapes like this had been seen before Tarkovsky but – I don't know how else to put it – their beingness had not been seen in this way. Tarkovsky reconfigured the world, brought this landscape – this way of seeing the world – into existence.[7]

It is this 'beingness' that marks the accounts of resurrection life in the Gospels. Telling details jump out: the head wrapping lying like a discarded chrysalis in the tomb; Jesus munching on a grilled fish; a sceptical disciple's finger hovering over the wound in Jesus' torso. Descriptions of unfolding events are spare and impressionistic. They overlap and separate out, sometimes reported in contradictory manner. Yet the feeling is not of narrative inconsistency but of the truth of this kind of experience of the new.

William Bridges, who writes better about human transitions than anyone, describes threshold experience like this: 'For many people, the experience of the neutral zone is essentially one of emptiness in which the old reality looks transparent and nothing feels solid anymore.'[8] What could be more transparent than a man passing through a wall? Than one who disappears from a table after breaking bread? Accepted reality has become disturbingly thin. I exaggerate, of course, because the Gospels detail anchors for the disciples, including a risen Lord and a reinterpretation of Old Testament Scripture underlining Jesus as the Son of God. Nevertheless, this feeling of immateriality pervades. One minute the risen Jesus is verifiably present, eating or inviting touch. The next he vanishes. In his new body, he is the same, yet he is also somehow different. He bears the marks of his crucifixion but travels unbounded by time or space.

Such metaphysical uncertainty is true to our experience of deep change. The new world is strangely familiar, yet entirely dissimilar. No wonder the disciples' responses are so erratic. No wonder that Christians through the centuries have reached out at such transitional times to accompanying guides and spiritual directors. No single follower of Jesus in the Gospels absorbs his rising in a moment of instant revelation. Mary is deceived by Jesus' appearance. The disciples believe that they're seeing a ghost. Thomas craves tangible evidence of the risen Jesus. Transformation is more progressive than instant. Over the forty days between Easter and the ascension, the disciples undergo a complex process of reimagining and reinterpreting recent events. They travel through stages of confusion, insight and further questioning. They fall back as often as they advance. Although they have 'found' the risen Jesus, much of the time they feel at a loss. We rarely enter a decisive new phase of life feeling adequate to the task.

Rebecca Solnit's *A Field Guide to Getting Lost* is a manual that the disciples would have done well to read. Solnit observes that when we experience deep change, we often feel lost. This lostness cuts two ways. We 'have lost' something, our old life, and grieve its disappearance. Yet we also 'are lost', beached, without a map or compass suitable for the new land in which we now find ourselves. 'Either way there is a loss of control,' she notes.[9] These are telling insights, true to the disciples' experience as well as our own. They point to the duality of threshold experience.

In liminal times, we struggle with the dissolution of the familiar, even as we open to this new time's emerging potential. Solnit writes that the etymology of 'lost' stems from the Old Norse *los*, a word describing an army's disbanding or the dismantling of a strategic formation.[10] When we're lost, the strategizing part of our mind falters. Our normal faculties of competency are veiled. Whereas we typically 'wage war' on life, strategically setting goals and marching on with heads held high, when we feel lost in life our strategic mind is forced to clear its desk and leave the premises. We require new faculties, such as close attention, intuition and listening. With our strategizing mind displaced, we can feel clumsy, lacking our usual skills for moving forward. The horizon may have opened up but the ground seems slender beneath our feet. Yet step forward we must as we begin to open up to this larger process. As described by Solnit, this is a journey through 'loss of control'. It is one mirrored in the post-resurrection narratives. While as readers we'd like to see the disciples rising to their new challenge, they are often lost in a fog of indecision. This is not a doctrinally neat or convenient recounting of events. It is, though, deeply human and spiritually and existentially true.

Let us now examine how different individuals respond to meeting the risen Jesus. Their stories will speak to each of us differently and to different moments in our change experience and discipleship. So much depends in this process on how we recognize new reality and whether we live it out wisely. With each of the four sets of people – Mary Magdalene, the two believers travelling to Emmaus, the cloistered disciples and Thomas – we observe a similar pattern. After the blinding despair of Good Friday and the long day's journey of the

Saturday, an un-blinding occurs. Each set of characters carries a faulty perception that the risen Jesus challenges.

Mary Magdalene initially mistakes the risen Jesus for an earthly gardener. Her clouded vision is principally the result of her grief. However, her grief is also paradoxically her entry point into new life. It is women who come first to the tomb and who most directly acknowledge their loss. In this, Mary exposes a difference that we often see between women and men as they navigate change. For Mary, this is firstly a relational issue. In John's Gospel, her tears precipitate supernatural revelation. She leans to look into the tomb and sees two angels. Her heartbreak opens the way for divine encounter. She is emotionally immersed in the moment, caught up in the rapids of change. Next, she stands weeping outside the tomb while Peter and John, unable to respond to her, run to tell the other disciples. For these two men, Jesus' apparent rising is more of a confounding puzzle to be reported and solved.

How often we see this divide in the different way that men and women respond to mid-life change. Women enter their grief for what has been lost and thereby clear the ground for the new to emerge. Their tears become not a point of termination but a first step calling new life into being. Such change, by contrast, can often be difficult for men whose identity and understanding are predicated on certainty, technology and lack of ambiguity. Mary remains present to the uncertainty of the moment; the two disciples recoil from it in alarm, perhaps still in denial of their grief. If we wish to understand the merits of Mary's way of being, we might simply note that her tears precede angelic encounter. Visiting the tomb of her loss and present to her grief, she moves on more swiftly than the two men to encounter the risen Jesus.

For her, as for us, new life manifests itself obliquely. Jesus does not appear before her in a blaze of glory. She turns round to see a stranger, surely the gardener. Jesus then intimately names her: 'Mary'. His tone instantly identifies him as her beloved Lord. Jesus has always cherished her name, in contrast to the many men in her life who have used her abusively. Naming and physical touch are two ways that we can honour a person's presence and innate dignity. It is no wonder that Mary seeks to reciprocate Jesus' intimate address with instinctive touch. However, as she makes to grasp Jesus, he counsels, 'Do not hold on to me, for I have not yet returned to the Father.' Risen life inhabits a transitional form. Jesus urges, 'Go instead to my brothers and tell them, "I am returning to my Father and your Father, to my God and your God"' (John 20:17). Mary never mistakes Jesus for a ghost, unlike the disciples in Luke's Gospel. Perhaps her lack of guilt precludes her from this anxiety and error. Nevertheless, Jesus is indiscriminate in his compassion. He does not condemn the disciples who abandoned him as traitors but names them as 'brothers'. He wants to reassure Mary and the disciples that they are his equals, in relationship like him with a loving Father.

We can read Jesus' command to Mary not to cling to him in two ways. First, he asks her to graduate from personal affection to more objective consideration. If she is the ex-prostitute figure of tradition for whom Jesus' containing, redemptive touch has been healing, he now announces the need for another dimension of relationship. Holding on to him, she cannot adequately prepare for the Spirit's coming. Until now, Jesus has only been present in his incarnate state to those he physically accompanies. Shortly, following his ascension and the Spirit's coming, he will be present to all believers, unlimited by time or space. He will no longer belong exclusively to those with whom he walks physically but to every believer on earth. Second, then, Mary will be able to 'hold' him indeed. She will herself be a holder for the Holy Spirit who is the Spirit of Jesus.

One beauty of Jesus' risen appearances is how they honour different ways in which different individuals need to encounter new spiritual life. Jesus' command to Mary not to cling contrasts with his invitation to Thomas to probe Jesus' wounds. What is the meaning of this apparent contradiction? Jesus acts differently to different people in his risen state. There is no fixed reality, or one size fits all, to this new life. It is as if Jesus asks: what does this person in front of me need in order to enter more deeply into the reality of my risen life? What does this person need to grasp what this new life means for him or her?

In renouncing her need to cling, Mary prepares for her subsequent reception of the Holy Spirit. She anticipates the change each disciple must make in advance of Pentecost. Jesus' resurrection sets the conditions for exalted, transformed life but one that the disciples will only start living out after the Spirit's coming. Before that, they must, in another death, let go of their former way of relating to Jesus. This explains why the risen Jesus spends forty days with them before his ascension. That time could be no shorter. He needs to move them beyond initial encounter into educational formation and adjusted relationship to him. They must die to how they have 'held' him in their minds and hearts until now. This constitutes a profound modification in their relationship.

An analogy might run like this. A husband develops prostate cancer. He elects to receive surgery for the removal of the cancerous cells. As a result of the operation, he is made impotent. Suddenly he and his wife have lost their sexual relationship of old. They must now discover intimacy in a whole new way. First, though, they need to grieve the loss of their previous sexual familiarity. Only then can they discover the fresh resources that they require for renewed intimacy. Their relationship remains fully intact but the means for living it out has changed. Any of us would find such a situation deeply challenging. What we would need, above all, is to know God's sustaining love and to experience the transforming balm of time. This is the consolatory aspect of these forty days between Easter Sunday and Jesus' ascension.

Mary and the women are able to stay present to their emotions. Jesus privileges them in showing himself to them first. Yet Luke's Gospel also depicts him reaching out to a pair of believers fleeing Jerusalem to drown their sorrows at Emmaus (or 'warm well'). God counsels us, 'Drink water from your own cistern, running water from your own well' (Proverbs 5:15). Sadly we often find it hard to stay put in a place of discomfort. We jump ship and run off to drink somewhere new when our lives turn desert.

The village of Emmaus may well have been a spa and certainly represents refuge from the painful aftermath of Jesus' crucifixion. These two are attempting to flee their shattered hopes. However, they are also 'talking with each other about everything that had happened' (Luke 24:14). Our attempts to escape painful reality often only intensify our need to make sense of it. Events of the last weeks have spelled incoherence and defeat for this pair. In their triumphalist interpretation of Old Testament prophecy, they anticipated a Messiah coming in glory and failed to absorb equivalent passages about his suffering. Onto this road comes Jesus, initially unrecognized by this pair in his risen state. If grief blinded Mary, desolation and false messianic expectations blind these two. Jesus, in his compassion, makes no distinction about whether Mary or they are worthier of encounter. Many of us, in his place, might have left this fugitive pair to despair and flight. Jesus, though, wants each one of us to encounter new life, however wrongly we may have reacted to the death of our cherished dreams.

It is instructive what Jesus does next. He invites this pair to describe their perception of the last three days. In doing so, they reveal their wholesale failure to understand his identity as the Son of God. Whereas Mary named Jesus 'Lord' when speaking to the angels in the tomb, this pair regard Jesus only as a prophet. First rebuking them (I suspect with a winsomely weary smile), he then offers them an unprecedented lesson in biblical interpretation under the open sky:

> He said to them, 'How foolish you are, and how slow of heart to believe all that the prophets have spoken! Did not the Christ have to suffer these things and then enter his glory?' And beginning with Moses and all the Prophets, he explained to them what was said in all the Scriptures concerning himself. (Luke 24:25–27)

Whereas Jesus needed to move Mary from impulsive affection to deliberate reflection, he needs to enlighten this pair about the connection between suffering and glory. So we too, on the threshold of new spiritual life, must allow false paradigms about our story to fall apart. These followers, like Mary, must begin to 'hold' Jesus in a fresh way.

Jesus first disarms these believers from asking misguided questions ('What was all *that* about?') and then guides them through a retrospective work of reinterpretation, preparing them for imminent revelation. As he speaks, he opens up new dimensions of hope. His Old Testament study reveals a Messiah who has come to bring salvation, a suffering servant whose death is not the end of a story but begins a new one for all humanity. What appeared to represent crushing defeat has actually been the realization of God's plan and the manifestation of his glory. So we too struggle with paschal change until we accept this paradox of transformation coming through suffering. When a secular society refuses the truth of this paradox, its citizens are robbed of resilience at the most basic psychological level. The risen Christ is utterly reshaping this pair's paradigmatic outlook. It is as if they and the disciples stood amid shattered shards of glass, in a scene of desolation. With a sudden shift of perspective, the glass shards now re-coalesce. The pair gaze up at a stained-glass window of insurmountable beauty.

It is significant how Jesus brings revelation. Initially in his Emmaus Bible class, he offers a cognitive reframing of recent events. He reinterprets Old Testament Scripture, bringing fresh, integrated understanding. In response, the pair's hearts burn in recognition. The risen Jesus will subsequently extend similar hermeneutical perspective to the disciples in Jerusalem. We need to pray for and covet such epiphanies of understanding through God's Word. In the months after my coming to faith, I desperately needed believing friends who would remind me of the promise of risen life and robustly ground my lived experience in Scripture. Transitioning into new life is not an act of the will or wilful boldness. It requires of us a perceptual, paradigmatic shift.

At the same time, crucial insight does not come for the pair until they experience the presence of the risen Christ. What follows then is a moment of grace equivalent to Mary's garden experience. There Jesus' soft voice roused Mary to her senses. Here the pair witness Jesus' nail-scarred hands, his breaking of bread, and his thanks and blessing. Hermeneutical understanding has formed the groundwork but the swift blow of revelation, almost felt like a violation, comes through God's presence. This alone rips the veil from his followers' eyes. This impact of physical reality will be replicated in many of the risen Jesus' encounters. It is his voice whispering in a garden, calling to the fishermen at sea, or his robust physical reality eating in a room or grilling fish by a shore, that bring revelation. I see this experience repeated among Alpha guests at St Aldates, Oxford. Early in the course, guests examine the historical reality of Jesus' existence and resurrection and consider the Bible as the word of God. However, it is on the course's awayday when we pray 'Come, Holy Spirit' that so many have a catalytic encounter with Christ. I think of a recent time when a young woman experienced a sense of Jesus standing behind her, cradling her in his love. For her, this was absolute confirmation of the living reality of his presence.

Such moments of divine encounter free us from any limited understanding that we are caught in meaningless change and apparent defeat. They reassure our soul that there is, in the words of C. S. Lewis, a 'deeper magic' at work. Reoriented and energized, the pair will hurry back to Jerusalem to share their illuminated understanding and experience. Jesus himself immediately disappears following this epiphany. On one level, as he said in Luke 22:15–16, he will only eat a Passover meal again when the kingdom of God comes in its fulfilment. His disappearance, though, repeated throughout the resurrection narratives, also permits us space and time to absorb such a startling paradigm shift. Jesus departs, leaving us only his absence, to meditate and reflect on what we have learned. It is a kindness of him and this new life. There is only so much reality that human beings can bear. We need times of encounter followed by times of reflection and reintegration.

Ronald Rolheiser sees the road to Emmaus as a symbol of our age, a type of our cultural moment.[11] For him, it speaks of our secular culture's pervasive anomie, the sense of disillusion with traditional vehicles that carried hope for previous generations. Faced with disillusion, our culture sets off down a barren, empty road with only temporary, palliative satisfaction at its end. This is not a journey to somewhere over the rainbow but a flight into fleeting consolation: a warm bath, a brief backrub. Yet, in his grace, Jesus meets us on this road. Despite our false suppositions and inconstancy, he gently challenges our disillusion by reawakening hope. At our invitation he turns from stranger to guest to host, and makes himself present with us.

We see another cultural type of our age in the locked room of huddled disciples in John 20:19. If Emmaus signifies the disillusion of taking flight, the locked room signifies a lying low in shame. The disciples feel as if they have failed and abandoned their master (as indeed they have), while their master has apparently abandoned them in death. They have lost all hope, and cower in hiding, fearful of the authorities. This speaks of anyone who has ever experienced a collapse in their belief system (whether Christian or not) and who feels unable to navigate the complex world outside. When our usual strategies collapse, we retreat or hide. Everything here smells of shame. These men have turned inwards and, apart from John and Peter, even resist the women's appeal to come to the empty tomb. Presumably they are sceptical or their fear of the authorities overrides their desire. In John's Gospel (we shall examine the more complex picture presented in Luke's Gospel in the next chapter), Jesus now arrives through locked doors to stand among them. Again, he is swift to show compassion, twice reassuring them ('Peace be with you!' John 20:19–21), and exhibiting his hands and side. He does everything in his power to draw his 'brothers' (v. 17) out of their shame – imparting love, not rebuke, enabling them to identify him by his scars, and thereby instilling joy as they realize that they are in the presence of the risen Lord.

Why does Scripture report his showing his wounds to them? The women at the tomb recognize him through sight or his voice. Scripture does not record Jesus' wounds in any account of their encounters. For the men, though, the wounds will be the conclusive proof. This again points to a difference in the way that men and women tend to process information. These men need concrete proof, while the women's recognition is more intuitive. It may be that Jesus also feels the need to reflect back to these hardened men his vulnerability as their saviour and their own woundedness. Women, whose bodies have already biologically been broken open through menstruation and birth, are in less need of such education.

Finally, in John's Gospel, Jesus announces, 'As the Father has sent me, I am sending you!' (20:21). He then breathes on his disciples, saying, 'Receive the Holy Spirit' (20:22). For generations, theologians have disagreed about this moment. Is this John's version of Pentecost, the coming of the Holy Spirit, or a prophetic pointer to that event? Certainly, in discipleship terms, this is less a moment of equipping than of calling. If this were an equipping, we have to ask why the disciples, as portrayed in John's Gospel, do not next demonstrate any of the confidence, initiative and activity that they will after Pentecost. Jesus is surely reiterating their calling, reinforcing how it will be accompanied by the Holy Spirit's guidance. The disciples' commissioning itself occurs at Pentecost when the Spirit comes in power and as a distinct person, not mediated through the breath of Christ. This interpretation speaks realistically of the experience of our spiritual lives. So often, the new believer or mature disciple passes through a paschal death and then breathes in fresh calling. Yet it takes time for that calling to be received and lived into. The time of commissioning and release comes later, after the person has grown in understanding and gained strengthening resources for the task ahead.

Thomas, in his encounter with the risen Jesus, typifies a different kind of response to spiritual new life. Thomas, we have learned, 'was not with the disciples when Jesus came' (John 20:24). We don't know why Thomas was absent, whether he had retreated in introspective isolation or felt unable to identify with his fellow disciples' beliefs. Whatever the reason, Thomas represents the radical individualist in each of us. He has heard at least four accounts of people whom he knows well having met the risen Jesus. However, he remains resistant to belief or new life. Thomas' absence from Jesus' previous appearance to the disciples has been seized on by preachers ever since. After the conversion of Evan Roberts, who would go on to be instrumental in the Welsh Revival of 1904–5, he would regularly walk a mile after work to attend Moriah Chapel. It was there one evening that he heard deacon William Davies exhort: 'Remember to be faithful. What if the Spirit descended and you were absent? Remember Thomas! What a loss he had!'[12] That night Evans set his heart on attending every prayer meeting and church service that he possibly could, repeating to himself, 'I will have the Spirit.'[13]

Thomas' separation from community informs his scepticism. For anthropologist Victor Turner, rites of passage are corporate events. The paradigm shift catalysed in a rite of passage demands mutual support and shared understanding. Today, many of us undergoing change can be separated from such a body of support. Consequently, we struggle to navigate our rite of passage in a healthy way. Trapped in an individualistic mindset, isolated and wounded, we hide away in locked rooms in shame. We lack the strong support and accountability of others who are on the same journey. This is why church is essential to our healthy formation. It is also the tremendous value of twelve-step groups, which provide authenticity and accountability as well as the support and wisdom of elders who have travelled a similar path. Thomas, like any isolated believer removed from the fire of community, begins to doubt and free-fall, a casualty of his isolation.

So it is that Jesus reappears, again reassures the disciples, 'Peace be with you!' (John 20:19, 21), and stands before Thomas, declaring: 'Put your finger here; see my hands. Reach out your hand and put it into my side. Stop doubting and believe' (John 20:27). What happens next has been largely shaped in our minds by Caravaggio's celebrated painting of this event.[14] We presume that Jesus guides Thomas' finger into his side, that Thomas discovers the corroborating evidence he needs and proclaims his statement of faith. I am not sure that this is correct. John never specifies whether Thomas reaches out his hand and touches Jesus or not. All that we do know is that, following Jesus' invitation, Thomas makes his great confession, 'My Lord and my God!' (John 20:28). It is, of course, entirely possible that Jesus provides the tangible evidence that Thomas' sceptical frame of mind requires. Such an interpretation of a hand plunged into a visible wound would honour the physicality of Jesus' resurrection as presented in the Gospels.

At the same time, might it be that the impact of Jesus' presence on Thomas is more relational than epistemological? Might it be that, as Jesus offers himself nakedly to his follower's touch, Thomas' defended heart and mind are disarmed by Jesus' intimacy and trust? This is his master, offering himself wholly through his wounds, just as Jesus has already given himself wholly through his wounds for Thomas on the cross. As Jesus shows his wounds, perhaps his implication to Thomas, like Joseph Beuys in his artwork, is 'show *your* wound', acknowledge your brokenness. Walter Brueggemann talks of the contrast between fidelity and certainty in ways insightful to this encounter:

> We all have a hunger for certitude. The problem is that the Gospel is not about certitude, it's about fidelity. So, what we all want to do, if we can, is immediately transpose fidelity into certitude, because fidelity is a relational category and certitude is a flat, mechanical category. So, we have to acknowledge our thirst for certitude, and then recognize that if you had all the certitudes in the world, it would not make the quality of your life any better because what we must have is fidelity.[15]

The disciples, post-resurrection, have no certainty about when Jesus will reappear to them. They do know, though, given his appearances, that he is wholly faithful to them. His standing before Thomas, I believe, is all that Thomas needs to have conviction and to declare Christ as his Lord and God. Jesus has been faithful to him. Jesus is here for Thomas, not just for his fellow disciples to whom Jesus appeared one week earlier. Thomas did not make things easier for himself by isolating himself from the disciples at that time. However, Jesus, as with the followers on the Emmaus road, holds no grudges and comes only in grace. As believers, we do not make things easier for ourselves if we become the dying coal that has fallen out of the fire. However, even there, lying on the cold floor, Jesus picks us up. He restores us to the fire of his love.

I once filmed an interview with Bishop Richard Chartres for an evangelistic course that the church in which I worshipped was developing. Pondering discipleship, Chartres mused, 'What is the greatest obstacle to our next conversion?' He paused, before intoning in his great bass voice, 'Our last conversion'. If discipleship is a series of continuing, ever deeper 'conversions', it is the influx of new life that frees us for further growth. Every one of our past spiritual breakthroughs ultimately becomes a prison. We need to know new paschal rising and to accept 'an invitation to grow even more'.[16] So often in threshold times we find it hard to trust the larger pattern. New life seems frighteningly transient. Previous securities run through our fingers like sand. Yet, from a future vantage point, we will eventually look back on every current event as part of a larger unfolding movement. What first seemed like dissonance, as in much contemporary atonal music, will resolve, from a future perspective, in symphonic unity.

Meanwhile, these gospel passages testify to how we can pass from death to life and find fresh hope with greatest grace: by mourning our losses, visiting the tombs of our disappointments, seeking new revelation in Scripture, remembering Christ in the breaking of bread, and keeping company in mutual support and encouragement. Practising these simple disciplines, astonishingly, new life comes.

'It is difficult to describe the neutral zone without speaking metaphorically . . . It is a strange no-man's-land between one world and the next. It is a world where you pick up mixed signals, some coming from the past and some from the future. Sometimes the signals jumble into noise, while at other times they cancel each other out, leaving only an eerie silence.'

William Bridges[1]

'A great call always has a great preparation.'

Ingrid Hansen[2]

6

Shaken

Until the disciples witness the risen Jesus with their own eyes, they are inoculated against the truth of his rising. They disbelieve other eyewitnesses. Only living encounter with Christ will cause the scales to fall from their eyes. This leaves them in a better place, one characterized by songwriter Leonard Cohen thus: 'It is good to be between a ruined house of bondage and a holy promised land.'[3] It is also a disorienting place. Luke writes that Jesus 'appeared to them over a period of forty days' (Acts 1:3), but in his Gospel John only records three appearances to them as a group. No single event like the crucifixion, resurrection, ascension or Pentecost dominates this phase. It consists more of a series of micro-moments punctuated by long gaps of time. William Bridges, transitions expert, describes this liminal phase in our lives as 'a time when it may seem that nothing is happening', 'a low-pressure area' and 'a long dark twilight that refuses to resolve itself into either real day or true night', where 'time slows down greatly'.[4] It can also be for the receptive person a richly teachable space, one that we have to get into to get out of the deadening prison of our former mindset. It can then become a fertile place of becoming, albeit only once we stop waiting for it to be over.

The phase lasts a protracted forty days because the disciples require time to transition in their understanding. Bridges helpfully contrasts change and transition:

> Change is situational. Transition, on the other hand, is psychological. It is not those events, but rather the inner reorientation and self-redefinition that you have to go through in order to incorporate any of those changes into your life. Without a transition, a change is just a rearrangement of the furniture. Unless transition happens, the change won't work, because it doesn't 'take'.[5]

Jesus asks the disciples to endure a complex series of transitions. Like the middle of a feature film, this liminal phase involves inner work and character growth rather than decisive outward action. Our old values system has crashed. We are in new territory. Caught in restless motion, we explore fresh avenues while our old selves flail in their death throes and yield to what is emerging.

Metaphorically, Jesus is engaging us in a new apprenticeship. In John 16:7, he declared: 'Unless I go away, the Counsellor will not come to you; but if I go, I will send him to you.' In this stage of discipleship, we prepare to receive Jesus' life in a different way. The disciples make ready for his departure in one form (his risen state) and his coming in another (the Holy Spirit). Marie de Hennezel identifies one aspect of Jesus' activity in describing her role in helping a dying patient let go of his former life:

> I'm a kind of human presence, out of time, able to release a flood of emotion in him. I am also someone who can just be there with

> him, without holding him back, without tying him down, the only person perhaps who can truly give him permission to die.[6]

In this guise, Jesus is the disciples' helper. However, he is also, of course, the risen Christ at whose rising they will necessarily celebrate, and he is the Christ shortly to ascend. Do the disciples need to become secure in the risen Jesus, to grieve his imminent departure or to anticipate his prospective coming in another form? The answer is all three. This produces an unstable medley of responses in them. Disorienting cross-currents of feeling swirl. No wonder that, on Jesus' appearing in the locked room, they do not simply erupt on to Jerusalem's streets in celebration. They are about to engage in a complex process of reorientation, re-education and re-formation.

By the time of Jesus' departure at his ascension, Luke depicts the disciples in a state of unequivocal joy ('they worshipped him and returned to Jerusalem with great joy', 24:52). The previous forty days, though, involve grieving as well as future anticipation. The disciples must relinquish the past, prepare for Jesus' departure and inhabit a place of new understanding. Only then will he commission them (Matthew 28:18–20). In this phase, outward activity is minimal but tension lurks beneath the surface. Jesus initiates change through his appearances, yet also then disappears outside the painting's frame. Negative space is as much a part of this phase as moments of epiphany and revelation. Above all, the disciples require generous time for transition.

It is an undesirable truth that any radical transition takes longer than we hope for or expect. We need 'forty days' to integrate complex shifts in our outer and inner worlds. Anyone who has experienced such a season will recognize the visceral truth of the metaphor of being caught in the belly of the beast. We can inwardly scream out for escape or relief through action. Resisting this is our greatest necessity. In this borderland, God patiently does his inner work. We discover deeper reserves. The liminal zone is not an obstacle to be circumvented but a place of potential insight. In this place, God prepares us for the Spirit-filled life that lies across the horizon. Embraced, this in-between place can prove to be the most formative place of becoming.

Theologians identify two dimensions to Jesus' activity in these forty days: he gives proof of his rising to a variety of followers, and instructs his disciples in the kingdom of God. As with the Emmaus followers, this involves fresh paradigmatic understanding:

> He said to them, 'This is what I told you while I was still with you: Everything must be fulfilled that is written about me in the Law of Moses, the Prophets and the Psalms.' Then he opened their minds so they could understand the Scriptures.
> (Luke 24:44–45)

Less pondered on is the *manner* in which Jesus relates to the disciples over this time: the fact that they experience both his presence and absence. The Gospels do not reveal his motives in this or the deepest metaphysical process in which he may be caught. Clearly, though, he is preparing his disciples for growth in a particular way. We can helpfully understand this is in terms of how any leader prepares followers for his or her succession. Poet David Whyte recounts a time as a young man working as a naturalist guide on a boat in the Galapagos Islands. Following the departure of Raphael, the boat's seasoned captain, an immature new captain's arrival set the stage for near disaster. One morning, Whyte awoke to rescue the boat from crashing into a cliff face. It had drifted from anchor in the night. The new captain had fallen asleep, impervious to danger. Raphael's brilliant leadership had lulled the crew into a lack of responsibility:

> Raphael had so filled his role of captain to capacity that we ourselves had become incapacitated in one crucial area: We had given up our own inner sense of captaincy. Somewhere inside us we had come to the decision that ultimate responsibility lay elsewhere . . . In the all-powerful presence of a great leader, it is easy to remain unaware of our own personal compass, a direction, a willingness to meet life unmediated by any cushioning parental presence.[7]

Jesus needs to prepare his followers for his disappearance as a leader; he therefore comes and goes over these forty days. He does not behave like a rescuer. He breaks past dependency as well as initiating his disciples into a new reality. He appears and imparts, then departs, forcing them to live in absence, reflection, waiting and adaptation. This discipleship phase, in short, is one of weaning. Jesus initiates this process in telling Mary Magdalene not to cling to him. Like a mother weaning her child, Jesus withholds what we want (things as they have been) and seeks to change our appetites. He shifts us from wanting him in one form (clinging) to another (the Spirit). This weaning is essential for our growth. We must prepare for a source of nourishment other than the incarnate or risen Jesus. His destiny lies at his Father's side. We must adapt, just as the child does with its weaning mother, coming to live in calmness with unfulfilled desires:

> I do not concern myself with great matters
> or things too wonderful for me.

> But I have stilled and quietened my soul;
>   like a weaned child with its mother,
>   like a weaned child is my soul within me.
> (Psalm 131:1–2)

To be weaned is to become mature. Jesus achieves this by withholding what we want while holding us close in his arms. His absences divest us of his continual presence. His presence reassures us of his continuing love for us in another form.

In the Jerusalem section of this phase, Jesus grows his disciples as leaders by developing their own sense of captaincy. In the second phase, he returns them to Galilee, the place of their first commitment. In Luke 24:5–6, the angels counsel the women at Jesus' tomb, 'Why do you look for the living among the dead? He is not here; he has risen!' We don't find new life in the grave, although there is no Easter Sunday without a Good Friday. The angel continues in Matthew 28:7: 'He has risen from the dead and is going ahead of you into Galilee. There you will see him.' The invitation is to return to the territory where Jesus first called the disciples, the starting point of their long obedience in the same direction.

When we suffer oppression and risk getting lost (as has been the case for the disciples in the spirituality of the Jerusalem phase), it is good to go back to the beginning. Jesus sends the disciples back to the place where they first thrilled to following him and saw God's power manifested in miraculous forms. Ronald Rolheiser brilliantly describes Galilee as not just 'a physical geography' but 'a place in the heart'. It is a territory where faith must be restored, where dreams that died at Golgotha can be received anew.[8] It is a territory that brings with it not just fresh sightings of the risen Jesus but new spiritual perceptions about his identity that have eluded his disciples until now. Galilee is the place where youthful dreams were forged and where broken dreams can be returned to the fire, to be hammered into a better shape. David Whyte, speaking of marriage, observes that 'marriage is where we have to be larger than the self who first made the vows'.[9] Returning to Galilee, we become larger than our younger self who first committed to Jesus.

The risen Jesus is our forerunner into Galilee. Here he reminds us of our initial conversion, chides our lukewarm or hardened hearts, and calls us into fresh dimensions of understanding. He reveals that the Jerusalem ministry, which, in the disciples' eyes, had seemed to go disastrously wrong, and the Galilean ministry where he acted with supernatural power were not a game of two halves but one continuous whole. Critically, he expands his teaching from the Emmaus followers, enlightening the disciples about God's kingdom and opening their eyes to his presence throughout Old Testament Scripture (Luke 24:44–45). They will spend some two-thirds of the forty-day period here in Galilee.

Galilee is the place where they will give Jesus back their hearts, as Peter does on the lake shore. This is a time for renewal and even, as with Peter, for forgiveness and restoration. So often on the threshold of new life we need to return to the old, the place of innocence, to gain perspective and evaluate our growth. At the end of Dickens' novel *Great Expectations*, Pip returns to Miss Havisham's derelict house, the starting point of his life journey. Here he meets Estella, his widowed childhood sweetheart, who reflects: 'Suffering has been stronger than all other teaching, and has taught me to understand what your heart used to be. I have been bent and broken but – I hope – into a better shape.'[10] In the house's shadow, Pip too understands the story of his life afresh. Returning to Galilee, we discover the difference between receiving Jesus' 'Follow me' with a novitiate's thrill of heart (as with Philip in John 1:43) and with a seasoned understanding (as with Peter in John 21:19). After Philip's youthful, and entirely essential, innocence, we witness Peter's mature appreciation of the dying to self and, for him, possible literal future death involved in true discipleship.

What resources can help us to navigate these 'forty days'? Spiritual directors, survival experts and Jesus' disciples might all agree on three things. The first is to become apprenticed to a necessary waiting in this territory. Liminal space generally feels like a waste of time. Our functional, goal-oriented natures chafe. Yet we must resist driven thinking, seeking to avoid vulnerability by pressing forward into a false competency. We must refuse to sabotage inner growth by accelerating into the future.

Second, we must agree fully to be present to this place. Laurence Gonzales, a survival expert, notes that people lost in wilderness situations too often fail to adjust their mental maps to their new reality. Without such an adjustment, 'You're carried along on your own story of yourself'.[11] That story may have sustained you in previous territories. Now, though, it risks irrelevance. We need to be in fresh conversation with our radically changed environment. The spiritual analogy is obvious. Touching on our need to relinquish habitual forms of support, as in weaning, Gonzales observes:

> One of the toughest steps a survivor has to take is to discard the hope of rescue, just as he discards the old world he left behind and accepts the new one. There is no other way for his brain to settle down. Although that idea seems paradoxical, it is essential . . . Dougal Robertson, who was cast away at sea for thirty-eight days, advised thinking of it this way: 'Rescue will come as a welcome interruption of . . . the survival voyage.'[12]

We must modify our inner maps and adjust to the new spiritual reality. It is no use harking back to the old or expecting Jesus' continuing presence. We must agree to not feeling lost. For we are not lost. We are simply somewhere new, right here and now. Does this constitute hopeless passivity? No, we must make healthy decisions in each moment. Does it necessitate striving? No, we must surrender to God's larger process. This is a crucible phase in which we allow God to bring our new selves into being. John Leach, analysing the liminal plight of those stranded in emergency situations, calls this the paradox of 'resignation without giving up. It is survival by surrender.'[13] Embraced, it leads to transformation and joyful participation in the sorrows of the world. We become part of a story larger than the imprisoning one that we had inhabited, and this fresh story yields its revelatory insights and bears us buoyantly forward.

Our third resource in this phase remains community: '"I'm going out to fish," Simon Peter told them, and they said, "We'll go with you"' (John 21:3). Between Gethsemane and Pentecost, the Gospel writers delineate little of the disciples' individual personalities. Yes, Thomas doubts and Peter seeks restoration. However, the stronger sense is of a collective pilgrim identity. The disciples are shaped and shape themselves in response to Christ's risen life. Anthropologist Victor Turner would see their being involved in a rite of passage. He writes of novices, or 'neophytes', in initiation rituals:

> It is as though they are being reduced or ground down to a uniform condition to be fashioned anew and endowed with additional powers to enable them to cope with their new station in life. Among themselves, neophytes tend to develop an intense comradeship and egalitarianism. Secular distinctions of rank and status disappear or are homogenized.[14]

The disciple who is personally humbled at an existential level is also linked in a tightly bonded community of support. Jesus' disciples no longer jockey for status. The Sons of Thunder remain mute. Instead, they discover a profounder comradeship than they have previously known. This bonding will strengthen them for their commission to convert, baptize, disciple and build up the early church. Dwelling in the present, then, actively surrendering to the here and now, and bonding in community: this is how wilderness survivors, neophytes and Christian disciples caught in a 'no man's land' endure, while opening themselves to growth by participating in a larger, emerging conversation.

Revisiting Galilee refreshes the disciples and enables them to measure their growth. However, a return to source can also return us to unfinished business and all that is spiritually unresolved. Of the lakeside meeting between Jesus and his disciples, John writes: 'This was now the third time Jesus appeared to his disciples after he was raised from the dead' (John 21:14). It forms his second personal encounter with Peter, the first having been alluded to in Luke 24:33–34. Only now, though, can Peter have the courageous conversation necessary following his denial. Despite the risen Jesus having earlier pointed to his wounds, proclaiming 'Peace' (John 20:19, 21) to indicate the Father's forgiveness possible through Jesus' sacrifice, Peter has remained in inner turmoil. Sometimes, it is we who cannot forgive ourselves. How this return to Galilee must have reminded Peter of his earlier vows of commitment to Jesus, all undermined on that night of denial after Christ's arrest. Mature seasons of life bring us up against places in our life where chickens come home to roost. Homecoming can be complex. For the prodigal son, it represents a spiritual return to belonging in the Father's arms. For the older brother, it exposes every place within himself where he has never come home.

The backdrop to Peter's conversation with Jesus appears to have been a testing stage in this forty-day phase. Biblical commentators debate whether the disciples' fishing in John 21 represents pragmatic activity or a flight into escape, analogous to the pair's journey to the Emmaus spa. Bruce Milne regards fishing as an ideal activity for the disciples after the emotional roller coaster of the last few weeks.[15] True, they need something tangible to do while waiting to be released into Jesus' great commission. To my mind, though, John's account suggests a backward drifting. Peter's declaration, 'I'm going out to fish', seems to arise from listlessness, and possibly even represents abandonment of his calling. Additionally, John writes that 'they went out and got into the boat, but that night they caught nothing' (21:3). The emphasis is on failure through self-willed activity, on lack of fruit. One's impression is that if Jesus didn't ascend, matters might atrophy further, with the disciples faltering until his next appearance.

They are struggling with their own autonomy, caught in Jesus' shadow, unable yet to step up in responsibility. Ingrid Hansen defines this as the trial of 'a season of waiting':

> The waiting itself is not the hard part. The hard part is to know what to do while you are waiting. Sometimes you don't even know what you are waiting for. You know there is a promise coming, but you do not know what it will look like when it arrives. You also do not know when it will arrive.[16]

Life can feel very unheroic in this phase. We sense the gap between a leader of magnetism, vision and authority and our deficiencies. These forty days and nights are often painfully ordinary, desperately protracted and embarrassingly endless. What temptation do we face in such times? To return to our old haunts: in this case, fishing. I think of a large church that I visited a short time ago. Once one of the jewels of the landscape of renewal, today this church lives in departed glory. It looks over its shoulder to the past. It is as if the colossus of a leader who steered it and brought renewal has not yet fully ascended. His followers kick their heels, perpetuating a conversation from twenty-five years ago. To their credit, they are busy at work fishing but the church displays little sign of life. I feel for them. I see their problem. They need to allow their former leader to ascend. They need to receive the Spirit for new vision and fresh equipping. Only then will they be free from their forty days of wandering. Only then will they witness and bear new life.

However, Jesus' disciples face a more immediate problem. The all-too-human leader of the future church, Peter, is suffering a dark night of the soul. His healing, as future master shepherd, is integral to the disciples' collective destiny. Only when he is restored will the disciples be ready for Jesus' ascension. This book is about spiritual growth. Human beings, though, can have an awkward attitude to growth, as the poet David Whyte intimates:

> Sometimes . . .
> I look out
> at everything
> growing so wild
> and faithfully beneath
> the sky
> and wonder
> why we are the one
> terrible
> part of creation
> privileged
> to refuse our flowering.[17]

During Jesus' ministry, we have witnessed Peter's growth and his refusal to flower in equal measure. Despite privately meeting the risen Jesus earlier, Peter hasn't yet initiated a courageous conversation about his denial. How true this is of our lives. For years we walk around, aware of issues beneath the surface of our everyday lives, withholding them from God. We need to graduate from being merely passionate, important though passion is to our faith, to focusing on growing in Christ, whatever the cost. Peter has always been passionate in his pursuit of Jesus. Just as he stepped out of a boat to walk on water, he plunges into the sea when Jesus calls to his disciples from the shore in John 21. So we too can plunge into 'doing church' and ceaseless ministry. We mature, however, when we graduate from plunging into persevering.

As a new Christian, I plunged into every available church activity. However, I failed to experience healing from my disordered years until I persevered. Pastoring, I meet many people whose lives have long been assailed with issues but who only address them when a life crisis strikes. Why wait? None of us knows what is over the horizon. We need a better way, cultivating hunger for spiritual growth. Peter's growth into persevering takes place because of an honest conversation that Jesus initiates. We heal when we step out from our walls, risk vulnerability, share with trusted others and bring our burdens to Jesus. This is one great test of spiritual maturity: to come out from defendedness and own our wounds. Doing this, we cooperate with God's purposes and enable our flowering.

In growth's most advanced phase we do not simply accept but embrace our flowering. Although it would be wonderful to ascribe this embracing phase to our hunger for growth, even here we may be driven by pragmatic response, as Elizabeth Appell observes acutely about deep change: 'And the day came when the risk to remain tight in a bud was more painful than the risk it took to blossom.'[18] Sometimes it becomes too painful not to grow. Since denying Jesus, Peter has been caught in a hinterland of self-condemnation. We might call this haunted time a desert, wilderness or winter. Yet when we treat this territory as a potential arena of revelation, God's grace can readily flow. How do we open ourselves to such revelation? First, we submit to the flinty realities of this harsh territory. Belden Lane, a connoisseur of desert territories, writes of the two questions posed to us by any wilderness: '"How much can you give up?" the desert asks. "And how much can you love?" Only in offering the severest answers to these two questions does one ever discover, at last, the solace of fierce landscapes.'[19]

Peter needs to do two things: give up his idealized self-image as Jesus' perfect follower and forfeit his self-love for love of Jesus' sheep. This is the New Testament model of the priest and pastor, someone unconstrained by self-imposed standards of impossible perfection, an undefended leader able to admit his own weakness: 'He is able to deal gently with those who are ignorant and are going astray, since he himself is subject to weakness. This is why he has to offer sacrifices for his own sins, as well as for the sins of the people' (Hebrews 5:2–3).

Jesus lovingly but forensically challenges Peter over two heart attitudes inhibiting his flowering. He must renounce both. Andrew Jones pinpoints these attitudes when he describes people whom he often meets while acting as a spiritual guide on pilgrimages:

> My experience with pilgrims has shown me how essential it is that they leave behind . . . regret and ambition. Harbouring regret prevents a person from moving on and ambition moves a person on too quickly from the opportunities of the present moment.[20]

Peter's regrets risk miring him in the past, like Epstein's sculpture *Lazarus* with its backward gaze still tethered to the tomb. Jesus' probing questions, spoken from a heart of love rather than draconian challenge, invite Peter into a fresh experience of God's generous grace. Ultimately, Peter's embrace of flowering is nothing to do with Peter himself, beside his availability for the conversation, and everything to do with Jesus' love. This is why we must never tire of upholding the message of grace:

> Grace is more than gifts. In grace something is overcome; grace occurs 'in spite of' something; grace occurs in spite of separation and estrangement. Grace is the reunion of life with life, the reconciliation of the self with itself. Grace is the acceptance of that which is rejected. Grace transforms fate into a meaningful destiny; it changes guilt into confidence and courage.[21]

The ambition of which Andrew Jones wrote we see in Peter's question to Jesus about John: 'Lord, what about him?' (John 21:21). Jesus has just alluded to Peter's future death as a martyr. Now Peter asks Jesus what John's fate will be. In the wake of his gracious restoration, these four words reveal a lingering fault line in Peter and a pervasive one in the collective male psyche. Peter's question speaks not only of ambition but also of competition with, even envy of, his fellow disciple. Envy often springs from a relative closeness of equals, as Freud observes: 'It is precisely the minor differences in people who are otherwise alike that form the basis of feelings of strangeness and hostility between them.'[22] Jesus knows that any lurking competitive ambition or envy threatens to derail Peter's future relationship with John and could be fatal for the health of the early church. Jesus therefore lances this final boil, his final recorded act of shepherding in John's Gospel.

John is the beloved disciple who enjoys mystical intimacy with Jesus. Peter is the passionate, gathering shepherd who will boldly proclaim the gospel and convert three thousand at Pentecost. One without the other is weak. A church can cultivate intimate appreciation of the presence of God but fail to look outwards. It can face outwards but fail to draw closer daily to God's heart. The church requires both seer and shepherd, just as we each need to know a spirituality of encounter with God and a spirituality of mission. Working in unity, Peter and John do remarkable things following Pentecost. All the evidence is of their close cooperation and complementarity (Acts 3:1; 4:3, 13, 19, 23). Jesus lances the wound of ambition and envy in Peter for his healing but also for the corporate flowering of the church. These two men must come together. Then, their differences will be not a tension but a source of increased strength. So we learn that our differences from fellow believers who are wired very differently from us are actually part of God's design – something to be embraced rather than experienced as a problem.

Therefore, the final lesson of this 'shaken' phase of discipleship is that God can't use us powerfully until we share courageously with him, admit our wounds and receive his healing. Calling is not necessarily defined in moments of mountain-top certainty. It may be received in acutest poverty of spirit. Remaining mute, Peter would have gone on to minister out of internal pessimism or a driven need to prove love for Jesus. Through this conversation, he is ready to receive a heart of flesh at the Holy Spirit's coming; he will go on to convert thousands and spread the gospel to the Gentiles. Without the conversation, there would have been a personal cost, his brokenness, but a far larger cost, Christ's church. Ultimately, healing in Christ isn't just a personal issue. It's a destiny issue. It involves not just our life but also the lives of countless others in God's kingdom. Today Jesus walks by your side and seeks your ear on a quiet shore. Talk honestly with him and experience his grace in any place of self-recrimination and unhealthy ambition. For when you do, you will know his healing and restoration. You will invite God's blessing on your life and that of others.

'We only really grasp the essence of another after he or she has gone away. When someone leaves us physically, we are given the chance to receive his or her presence in a deeper way.'
Ronald Rolheiser[1]

'WILLIAM: "When Che died, Fidel wept; but in that speech where he wept, he was saying that Che hadn't died . . . He was a seed fallen to the ground. Che dead is more dangerous than Che alive."
FELIPE: "Because now he's not just Che."
WILLIAM: "And his death, by God, cast his shadow over the whole world!"
FELIPE: "Now Che dead isn't just Che; his spirit exists in many Ches."
BOSCO: "There's a bunch of Ches, thousands of Ches."'
Ernesto Cardenal[2]

'Then the man said, "Let me go, for it is daybreak." But Jacob replied, "I will not let you go unless you bless me."'
Genesis 32:26

7

Blessed

The ascension represents the end of our forty-day apprenticeship. We reach the frontier of one borderland to find ourselves poised at a new threshold. C. S. Lewis compresses the essence of Jesus' ascension in a thrillingly descriptive metaphor:

> In the Christian story God descends to re-ascend. He comes down; down from the heights of absolute being into time and space, down into humanity . . . down to the very roots and seabed of the Nature He has created. But He goes down to come up again and bring the whole ruined world up with Him . . . One may think of a diver, first reducing himself to nakedness, then glancing in mid-air, then gone with a splash, vanished, rushing down through green and warm water into black and cold water, down through increasing pressure into the death-like regions of ooze and slime and old decay; then up again, back to colour and light, his lungs almost bursting, till suddenly he breaks surface again, holding in his hand the dripping, precious thing that he went down to recover.[3]

In Lewis's metaphor, the diver's starting point is in the heavenly heights. From here he plunges down to retrieve the buried pearl and it is to here that he returns, triumphant. At the ascension, Jesus carries fallen humanity, his pearl, up into heaven. The disciples will know that they are now seated with him in heavenly places. No wonder that their joy overflows. No wonder that their grieving is over. Their life is now 'hidden with Christ in God' (Colossians 3:3). Andrew Murray rightly registers this phase as a tipping point in our discipleship journey: 'The knowledge of Jesus as having entered heaven for us, and taken us in union with Himself into a heavenly life is what will deliver the Christian from all that is low and feeble, and lift him to a life of joy and strength.'[4]

For Jesus' own perspective on his ascension, we have his words in John 16:7–8:

> But I tell you the truth: It is for your good that I am going away. Unless I go away, the Counsellor will not come to you; but if I go, I will send him to you. When he comes, he will convict the world of guilt in regard to sin and righteousness and judgment.

Jesus' astonishing claim is that his departure from the disciples, after three unforgettable years with him, is for their advantage. Only through his departing will the Holy Spirit come, indwelling and blessing those left behind. This is not easy for the disciples to accept and integrate as truth, even if they hypothetically understand it. Jesus insists that they will know greater blessing through his absence than his presence. Although he will have gone, he will be more fully present across the entire earth. The disciples already contain the seed of the Spirit for new life within them. Jesus imparted it to them when he breathed on them. However, they will only fully receive his intensified presence once he has departed. Then the breath of the Spirit will come from heaven itself, sweeping through their midst like a mighty wind, as it does at Pentecost.

The ascension signals the inauguration of Jesus' heavenly reign. Far from its leading the disciples to unseemly self-promotion or competition, it impresses on them their human, creaturely status. They are co-equal subjects of an ascended King. Any talk of who is to sit by Jesus' side evaporates entirely, never to be repeated again. After their preparatory forty days, they grasp that Jesus' heavenly enthronement marks the completion of his earthly ministry and the commencement of his heavenly one. As theologian Abraham Kuyper says, 'There is not a square inch in the whole domain of our human existence over which Christ, who is Sovereign over all, does not cry, "Mine!"'[5] Although Jesus' enemies are not yet fully subject to him, and will be so only at his return, his eternal reign has begun. Moreover, that reign also involves us as his earthly subjects in continuing his mission upon earth. The start of his heavenly ministry thus inaugurates the full dimensions of the disciples' earthly ministry. In Ephesians 4:8 (NIV 2011), Paul describes how, as King, Jesus also gives 'gifts to his people' to empower them in office. In addition, Jesus becomes our heavenly High Priest, carrying our wounds to God and petitioning for the forgiveness of our sins. We can delight in knowing his proximity to God and that he petitions the Father on our behalf.

This theology, exhilarating as it is, does not mean that this stage of spiritual growth is simple. The ascension brings to a head spiritual and psychological challenges that the disciples have faced during the last forty days. Their first challenge is whether they are ready to let the risen Jesus ascend. Any ascension depends on our being ready to let the dead person go. Only when a person is allowed to ascend can they bless us, as Jesus does, in their parting. I have seen people distraught at a loved one's untimely death, hysterical in hospital car parks as they arrive to identify the body. They cannot yet face the reality of the loved one's death. They are certainly not near to letting him or her ascend. That will come later. Conversely, I have accompanied people over the months or years of a loved one's lingering illness and fading. Well prepared for what is coming, such people can often let the loved one die and ascend in swift succession.

My father died unexpectedly when I was twenty-three. However, given my immaturity at the time and my obtuseness in processing his death well, it was another eighteen years before I felt that he could bless me in his parting. Ascension is the point at which we allow a person fully to ascend. They leave, as they already have done in death, but now we co-operate in their parting. The distinct moment of receiving my father's blessing came those years later when, visiting the place where his ashes are scattered, I pondered on how I might find a woman with whom I could fall in love and marry. I suddenly sensed my father's reply, as I received specific thoughts of counsel and felt released from faulty vision. Henri Nouwen underlines the importance of the person's 'ascending' for everything that will follow in the paschal cycle of transformation:

> The deaths of those whom we love and who love us, open up the possibility of a new, more radical communion, a new intimacy, a new belonging to each other. If love is, indeed, stronger than death, then death has the potential to deepen and strengthen the bonds of love. It was only after Jesus had left his disciples that they were able to grasp what he truly meant to them. But isn't that true for all who die in love?
>
> It is only when we have died that our spirits can completely reveal themselves.[6]

For this revelation, the disciples must let Jesus ascend. Spurgeon, in a brilliant insight, points out that prior to the ascension, the disciples leave Jerusalem and travel towards Bethany where they last saw the dead Lazarus rise. Jesus' command to them about Lazarus at that time was an instruction to free the reawakened man from his grave clothes: 'Loose him, and let him go' (John 11:44, KJV). Now once again they have to loose someone and let them go. This time that person is their master, Jesus.

The second challenge that the disciples face as their apprenticeship ends is whether they are ready for the responsibility of leadership. The failure or departure of any leader crystallizes this issue. Earlier we saw how a youthful David Whyte in the Galapagos Islands discovered the limits of his ship's new captain. At such moments:

> We are orphaned from a familiar parent–child relationship but we are also, if we can rise to the occasion, thankfully emancipated. We are ushered into an adult–adult conversation with our own powers. Something must be done. We must speak out, take the wheel, call the rest of the crew members ourselves.[7]

However well Jesus prepared the disciples in the forty-day phase, the ultimate removal of a cushioning parental presence is always unsettling. This has represented part of the disciples' drama during the weaning time: anxiety at assuming a captaincy so masterfully inhabited by Jesus. Laurence Gonzales, an expert in survival psychology, remembering following a bushcraft guide into deep woodland, touches on the existential challenge of retaining our autonomy in the presence of a powerfully capable leader:

> After we'd followed him deep into the woods, he asked us to close our eyes and point the way home. It is a humbling experience to

> find that you can't. I'd been following him, which is never a good idea. I had not walked my own walk, and as a result, I was lost.[8]

Jesus knows the dangers of slavish following. In his ministry, he has encouraged his disciples to submit to his authority *and* know a rightful independence. Often absent since his resurrection, he has sought to free them from overdependency. Our danger as disciples is always to substitute adherence to rules and works for Jesus' liberating discipleship. The Pharisees embody slavish observation of rules with terrifying absoluteness, symbolizing human anxiety at uncertainty. In his ascension, Jesus invites his disciples to meet life with their own sense of direction, unmediated by his shielding presence. They can do so willingly because they have submitted to his spirituality of weaning, now complete in God's perfect timing.

The Great Commission in Matthew's Gospel (28:18–20) represents the moment when Jesus says, 'It is now up to you.' As such, he provides a perfect balance of commanding mandate and ministerial authority along with pastoral assurance of supernatural assistance and comfort: 'And surely I am with you always, to the very end of the age' (28:20). To the fulfilment of God's plans in human history, Jesus will be Emmanuel, God with us, in every moment. The disciples know that they now stand on the threshold of new responsibility (a potential spur to anxiety) but are assured of Jesus' delegated authority and companioning presence. He is giving them space to do the impossible. He is freeing them from his shadow while generously offering a gift that will bring full enabling. Thus he says that he will send the Spirit in power and will work with them in a beautiful new way. The lesson for our discipleship is to allow old life to ascend in confidence, knowing that Jesus endows us with his authority for all time to come.

The disciples must learn two additional lessons before receiving Jesus' blessing. Each constitutes a challenge regarding how to move forward into new life. Consider an analogy for their first lesson, drawn from my theatre directing career. In my twenties, auditioning actors in their mid-forties for touring Shakespeare productions, I would often encounter men who had crossed the threshold of forty, only to realize that their youthful dreams of stardom had failed. Those unable to accept the death of their dreams sank into jaundiced cynicism or buried their sorrows in drink. Those prepared to look sober reality in the face would sometimes falter and disappear for a few years, lost off casting directors' radar, before resurrecting their career in their fifties, humbled, sage and more accommodating to the contingencies of the world. Allowing our old dreams to depart before they become compulsive fantasies is intrinsic to human maturing. We need to let unsustainable dreams go if bitterness is not to engulf us when we fail to leap over the rainbow or turn back the clock to a kinder time.

The false dream to which the disciples still cling before the ascension, and which Jesus will insist they relinquish, is of an all-conquering Messiah who will reconfigure political reality. To their question about when Jesus is going to restore the kingdom to Israel, he firmly slaps them down: 'It is not for you to know the times or dates the Father has set by his own authority' (Acts 1:7). With this sentence, Jesus ends their political fantasies and we hear no more about them from this time on. This does not mean that God's rule does not exist on earth. Jesus' ministry has already confirmed that God's kingdom is at hand. It does mean, though, that God's kingdom is not about political activism. Jesus curtly dispels any worldly fantasy of changing the earth through pulling political levers.

This represents a tempering of simplistic activism. At university I rejected Christianity for the radical politics of the

German playwright Bertolt Brecht. Railing against a Christian God whom I felt to be passive in permitting suffering, I embraced Brecht's Marxist politics, which, I believed, sought to address suffering's systemic roots. My blindness was twofold. First, my critique of God's apparent imperviousness to suffering, pronounced as objective argument, actually sprang from personal alienation. Second, I lay the blame for all injustice at God's door, choosing to ignore his frequent exhortations for justice in Scripture. Like Jesus' callow disciples, I needed to come out of simplistic ideas about securing human change. Deep spiritual change addresses the problem of the human heart underlying injustice issues and is nothing to do with our self-willed activity. Instead, it has everything to do with the Holy Spirit's power in enabling us faithfully to witness to Christ: 'But you will receive power when the Holy Spirit comes on you; and you will be my witnesses in Jerusalem, and in all Judea and Samaria, and to the ends of the earth' (Acts 1:8). Jesus implies we had better not substitute our agenda for his. He exhorts us to witness to him, including his refusal of political activism as a primary instrument of change. It is not that politics isn't an entirely legitimate sphere of activity for a Christian to enter. It is simply not to be seen as synonymous with the subtler dynamics of God's kingdom.

The second lesson involves the disciples coming out of speculative fantasy about the heavenly Jesus. After becoming disenchanted with Brecht's politics in my late twenties, I travelled to the other extreme, engaging in over-etherealized New Age thinking. This consisted in my exploring various Eastern spiritualities, self-help movements and meditation practices. I came to believe that the answer to personal and corporate change lay not in politics but in some kind of radical enlargement of humanity's spiritual consciousness. Although I now shudder at my naivety, it represented another youthful attempt to imagine change. This is so often the way with us when we are young and long to work for a better world. How, then, does Jesus warn his disciples of this particular danger of abstracted spirituality? He does so through the two angels who, following his ascension, draw the disciples' eyes back from heaven to earth:

> They were looking intently up into sky the as he was going, when suddenly two men dressed in white stood beside them. 'Men of Galilee,' they said, 'why do you stand here looking into the sky? This same Jesus, who has been taken from you into heaven, will come back in the same way you have seen him go into heaven.' (Acts 1:10–11)

Angels appear at both Jesus' resurrection and ascension. In each case, God sends supernatural agents to help the disciples across a necessary threshold. On Easter Sunday, their presence lifted the disciples out of earthly depression into the supernatural reality of Christ's rising. Here, their appearance, by contrast, earths the disciples and diverts them from fixating on heaven. In each case, human beings have to recognize, in humility, that they are unequal to the events they are witnessing. In the presence of God's powerful activity, they need supernatural counsel to understand what is going on. While the disciples stand, open-mouthed, gazing upwards, the angels reproach them for being too long amazed. They dispassionately break the current emotional continuum between the disciples and the ascended Jesus, announcing the certainty of his future return. In short, they interpret the disciples' spiritual experience, refocusing them from lofty pietism to earthly mission.

Whenever we experience heaven open, we risk remaining fixated on our spiritual experience, craving its repetition. We require grounded guides to earth us again. A short time ago, during the ministry time at a conference, God blessed me with a 'sighting' of his heavenly glory. Filled afresh with the Spirit, with eyes closed but seeing in my mind's eye a brilliant light streaming down on me, I found my arms involuntarily stretching upwards, as if my spirit was straining to reach heaven. Some days later I confided to my wife that earthly reality, by contrast, felt depressing. A strong part of me still longed for eternity, even to be taken up from this life. My wife was understandably alarmed. It took a sobering conversation with two gifted spiritual counsellors for me to see that I needed to repent. God's purpose in granting me this vision was not to idolize the experience or fixate on eternity to the cost of this world. It was that this experience should inform my theology, ministry and witness as long as God has purposes for me here on earth.

The angels return the disciples to their commission. Our charge is not to linger in visions of a heavenly home but to translate this reality into ministry to a hurting world. God imparts visions of glory to recalibrate our earthly faith. Spiritual experience can be electrifying, but with such a voltage passing through us we require a solid grounding system to earth the current. The angels tell us not to engage in fruitless speculation about Jesus' heavenly activity or his return but to play our part in bearing new life.

Today we continue to see these dual temptations (to come out of political fantasy about the kingdom of God and to resist lingering in heavenly fantasy and pietism) in action. In the run-up to Nelson Mandela's death in 2013, the black community in South Africa struggled to accept his imminent departure. During his illness, the community desperately sought to will him back to life. Nevertheless, his final leaving was inevitable. The only question was when the community would be able to let him go and ascend. Only then would they be able to receive the spirit that he longed to bequeath to them. Their temptation was either to resort to the kind of political agitation that Mandela refused or to gaze wistfully after him in death, wishing naively for his return. Today, the world waits to see how South Africa will move forward, either empowered by Mandela's spirit, or undermined by conflicted elements latent in the national psyche. In the cultural imagination, Mandela has gone to glory. We wait to see if South Africans can fully receive and embody his spirit, living similar lives of generous sacrifice.

The third question that the ascension poses is whether we are ready to allow the departing person's life to bless us. This is not as simple as it sounds. A person's sudden death in unexpected circumstances can be traumatic. Properly prepared for, though, a person's dying yields blessing. So it is with Jesus who, in his ascension, bequeaths us a spiritual model for dying and ascending. For Henri Nouwen, the dying Christian needs to trust that he has a spirit to send that will bring life to those that he is leaving. Viewed thus, death becomes a way of conferring ourselves as a final gift:

> You and I have to trust that our short little lives can bear fruit far beyond the boundaries of our chronologies . . . We often see or feel only the dying, but the harvest will be abundant even when we ourselves are not the harvesters.[9]

On the Mount of Olives at his ascension, Jesus 'lifted up his hands and blessed them. While he was blessing them, he left them and was taken up into heaven' (Luke 24:50–51). Jesus continually blesses his disciples as he leaves this life. Their joy in returning to Jerusalem springs entirely from their having fully received his blessing. On this Mount, not far from Gethsemane where Jesus accepted his Father's commission, the disciples accept Jesus' mandate for their future lives. The circle of Christ's Gethsemane 'Yes' is drawn tight in their embrace of his commission for them. They have completed their necessary spiritual business. Hence, they can release Jesus to ascend and freely absorb his blessing. Only when we let the old life ascend do we create space to receive its legacy for new life. However, to understand why Jesus' blessing represents such a turning point for the disciples, we must probe a theology of blessing more deeply.

Blessing has a threefold dimension in Christian discipleship. Ronald Rolheiser locates the first dimension in the etymology of 'blessing' – 'speaking well' of a person, giving away some of your highest life so that another may have more of it in their life.[10] We all need to be seen, known and told that we are beloved and significant. That God blessed Jesus in this way at his baptism speaks of the foundational importance of this human need. Jesus' disciples require his validation at his ascension, just as any soldiers require their leader's 'Yes' before embarking on a challenging mission. The disciples need Jesus' 'I believe in you' because their beloved master is departing the earth. Left alone, it is vital that they know that he has left part of himself, his approval, with them.

Second, blessing signifies anointing. The disciples on the Mount of Olives stand at a new threshold. As Jesus ascends, they see divine traffic between earth and heaven, recalling Jacob's dream of angels ascending and descending in Genesis 28:12. This open heaven signals arrival at another liminal moment in their lives. Margaret Silf describes the metaphorical importance of blessing as anointing to threshold experience:

> It blesses the transition across the boundary. It eases the passage through fear and loneliness, by lubricating the way with love. Above all, it speaks the truth of our hearts, that this place of

> passing is sacred space and that the person being anointed is moving beyond the known and the limited, into the unknown and the infinite.[11]

The disciples are graduating to a new level of spiritual experience. Jesus anoints them as he departs. He pours the oil of blessing on their heads, the great High Priest anointing his priests for future service. We need God's anointing as we step into new dimensions of earthly ministry.

The last dimension of blessing is empowering. Today, all too often failing to grasp the naturally supernatural kingdom in which we live, we reduce blessing to a form of 'wishing well', even something condescending, as when we wryly remark, 'Bless!' This could not be further from the potent virility of Jesus' blessing. The last thing that the disciples need is some polite farewell; they require divine infusing and empowering: 'Unless the LORD builds the house, its builders labour in vain' (Psalm 127:1). Without his blessing, the disciples would likely labour in their strength rather than lean on God in humble dependency. When Peter preaches on Pentecost, this rough-tongued, impulsive fisherman will see God move because he has received Jesus' blessing and the Holy Spirit. We desperately need the Lord to build the house. Without his blessing, we flounder in merely human schemes.

Biblically, blessing is not always our prerogative. However, it is something for which we can wrestle. Jacob has to wrestle for God's blessing. In the forty days since Easter, the disciples, though disoriented, have cleaved to Jesus and tenaciously extracted every lesson that they need from him. Like Jacob (Genesis 32:26), they have implicitly demanded, 'We will not let you go unless you bless us.' They need his blessing because, without it, they know that their ministry will be fruitless. It is their ability fully to receive his blessing that tips their scales to joy. Moreover, Luke clarifies that this is not just a mountain-top joy but one that endures in them on their return to Jerusalem (Luke 24:52) where they have known such recent oppression and Christ's suffering. We too must wrestle for blessing in the valleys if we wish to go forward with joy.

To see all the different threads of ascension spirituality gathered in one constellating example, we can turn to a poem, 'Farewell Letter', by David Whyte, written after his beloved mother's death.[12] In it the poet's imagination stretches to contemplate something much larger than his own individual loss:

She wrote me a letter
after her death,
and I remember
a kind of happy light
falling on the envelope
as I sat by the rose tree,
on her old bench
at the back door,
so surprised by its arrival,
wondering what she would say
looking up before I could open it
and laughing to myself
in silent expectation.

Dear son, it is time
for me to leave you.
I am afraid that the words
you are used to hearing
are no longer mine to give,
they are gone and mingled
back in the world

where it is no longer
in my power
to be their first
original author
nor their last
loving bearer.
You can hear
motherly
words of affection now
only from your own mouth
and only
when you speak them
to those
who stand
motherless
before you.

As for me I must forsake
adulthood
and be bound gladly
to a new childhood.
You must understand
this apprenticeship
demands of me
an elemental innocence
from everything
I ever held in my hands.
I know your generous soul
is well able to let me go,
you will in the end
be happy to know
my God was true
and I find myself

after loving you all so long,
in the wide,
infinite mercy
of being mothered myself.

P.S. All of your intuitions were true.

Whyte senses his ascended mother apprenticed to a new childhood. She has forsaken her earthly mothering. Now God holds her in *his* mothering embrace. However, there is not just a new calling on her. There is also one on her son who must now speak motherly words to any who stand motherless before him. So often, we begin to embody the deepest characteristics of a beloved mentor or parent only after they die and we take up the responsibility to carry on the work of their spirit. Whyte's mother invokes his generosity to release her into her new childhood. In the same way, she opens up for him a new work of comforting others. That is her loving spirit's legacy.

Sometimes ascension's fruit is first seen at funerals or memorial services. Recently, the death of a beloved member of our church occasioned a significant outpouring of grief. At her memorial service, family and friends celebrated her extravagant hospitality and love for others. One could tangibly sense the desire of those gathered to assimilate her qualities into their lives. This cherished woman was bequeathing her spirit and we were yearning to receive and embody it. Sometimes it is only with a person's ascension that we begin to incorporate the fruit of their life into our own.

Ascension represents a spiritual mystery. The forty days since Easter have demanded intense inner preparatory work from the disciples. At this boundary, though, God sends angels to 'carry us over'. As Joseph Beuys said of his healing while staying with the two brothers on their farm, 'There is much that helps us – not just people.'[13] David Whyte observes about the alchemy of spiritual growth represented at such times:

> You actually don't do the willful work of transformation . . . You put yourself in conversations, you put yourself in edges between this and that, and you crack your heart just a little bit, and let the wind get behind the door and blow it open.[14]

The ascension catalytically changes the disciples, to an extent unparalleled so far in the paschal narrative. Even the resurrection did not precipitate such immediate, pivotal transformation. Receiving Jesus' blessing as he ascends 'scattering promises of power', as Inkling Charles Williams puts it, the disciples praise and bless him:[15] 'Then they worshipped him and returned to Jerusalem with great joy. And they stayed continually at the temple, praising God' (Luke 24:52–53).

Jesus' ascension ends the shame-ridden hiding the disciples have known since Gethsemane. They step out of the shadows and reclaim their place in the temple. They return to the public stage. Now is a time to wait for everything marvellous that has been promised. So we too, when we grasp Christ as seated in heavenly places, can be released from inertia into transformative activity in public life. Reconciled with the Father, rejoicing in the new proximity of Father and Son, we need only the further empowering that Jesus has promised. For forty days we have wandered in wilderness, shaken, requiring re-education and re-formation. At Christ's ascension, we celebrate his glorious coronation as King. What will follow are ten days that end up shaking the world.

'Only where the Spirit is sighed, cried, and prayed for does he become present and newly active.'
Karl Barth[1]

'The Cinderella of the church of today is the prayer meeting. This handmaid of the Lord is unloved and unwooed because she is not dripping with the pearls of intellectualism, nor glamorous with the silks of philosophy; neither is she enchanting with the tiara of psychology. She wears the homespuns of sincerity and humility and so is not afraid to kneel!'
Leonard Ravenhill[2]

'Pentecost happened at a meeting! One of the central events that shaped Christian history and history in general, happened not to an individual off praying alone . . . It happened to a community, to a church congregation assembled for prayer, to a family of faith gathered to wait for God's guidance.'
Ronald Rolheiser[3]

8
Begging

The ascension catalyses the disciples' spiritual lives, as it must do ours. Too often as Christians we remain marooned in the hinterland between Ascension and Pentecost. We believe in the resurrection and ascension but live out of touch with their animating power. Doctrinally we rest on secure foundations but experientially we lack God's Spirit for renewed life. To counter this, we need to yearn for the Holy Spirit, not giving up in dissatisfaction because of unsatisfied thirst but actively seeking quenching. This is the inner restlessness and desire that Oswald Chambers records in his diary:

> The Holy Spirit must anoint me for the work, fire me, and so vividly convince me that such and such a way is mine to aim at, or I shall not go, I will not, I dare not . . . Here is the lamb and the wood, but where is the fire? Nothing but the fire of the most Holy Spirit of God can make the offering holy and unblameable and acceptable in His sight.[4]

Thankfully, the disciples' hungering for the Holy Spirit after the ascension provides a more compelling model for our discipleship than any aspect of their behaviour since Gethsemane. Luke describes them as filled with 'great joy' (Luke 24:51). They have witnessed heaven's opening and understood Jesus' rising from death and ascent to glory as representing the hinge of history. The bridegroom sits at the Father's right hand and it only remains for the bride to prepare for her wedding day on his return. Part of her preparation will involve her growth in character, as we will see fulfilled in the disciples' humble, assiduous asking over the next ten days. Part of it will involve her being clothed with power from on high. A bride requires both maturity of character and appropriate clothing for the hour when the bridegroom arrives to stand by her side.

We might note two introductory points regarding this ten-day period of 'begging'. First, following the presence of angels on Easter Sunday and at the ascension, we now find an absence of intervention by any supernatural agents. This is a very human period of preparation, preceding the most collective supernatural manifestation so far in the New Testament: the release of the Holy Spirit. Just as the four Gospels now funnel into the single account of Acts, so the disciples are caught in a time of spiritual convergence.

Second, this 'begging' phase involves the disciples in their most disciplined waiting yet. In contrast to their acerbic rivalries and impetuosity during Jesus' three years of ministry, they now embrace patience, refusing to seek to precipitate any manifestation of the Holy Spirit. Their manner speaks of how we are to prepare prayerfully in this phase of spiritual growth. This is a time not of complacent inactivity or respectful quiescence but of intense spiritual work, albeit subsumed within God's sovereign timing for the Holy Spirit's release. As one might say about the creative process, we work to get inspired, we don't get inspired to work. The disciples move beyond their reactive pose adopted since Gethsemane to become protagonists who maturely wait in worship and prayer.

In Luke 24:49, Jesus declares before his ascension, 'I am going to send you what my Father has promised; but stay in the city until you have been clothed with power from on high.' Although Jerusalem has been a place of contestation in Jesus' ministry, it is to the city, not to Galilee, that he directs his disciples to return. Jerusalem is foundational to his purposes. God is present there, even amid contestation. Indeed, God has revealed his glory in the place of Christ's deepest suffering. Where God strongly manifests his presence, we should expect contestation. Jesus' direction for his disciples to return to Jerusalem speaks of cities' strategic capital in a way encouraging for those of us ministering in crossroads cities. I recently met a church leader researching the twelve most strategic capital cities current in the world, with a view to planting from his church in each of these places of influence. Is this grandiosity or, as I prefer to think, apostolic vision recognizing the importance of cities in God's sovereign plan? Certainly the Holy Spirit will come at this time not in the spa setting of Emmaus but in the midst of a noisy, bustling, argumentative city – just as the Spirit comes in the midst of Oxford today.

At the same time, the disciples find a place of retreat within this hectic city. Although they also worship in the temple in Luke's Gospel, Acts spotlights their ten-day gathering in the upper room. They retire into a cloistered place, incubation being key to this discipleship stage. Just as Jesus retreated from crowds to quiet places, so the disciples enter a cocooned space as part of their growth:

> The chrysalis stage of faith is an intensely private and internal phase because what is emerging is initially fragile and vulnerable . . . We therefore need a spacious space, a protective space and a space that keeps us connected to the heart of Christian faith.[5]

Where the cave of Gethsemane was a place of captivity and unconsciousness, the upper room releases the disciples into fresh consciousness. In ritual terms, it is the cave to which the liminal acolyte retires to forsake social obligations and engage with deeper spiritual realities. Arnold Toynbee, writing of the pattern of spiritual development, characterizes this as a phase of 'withdrawal' preceding one of 'return'.[6] He describes how the 'anchorite' (Greek: 'one who goes apart') steps out of the world to seek transfiguration, only to return to bless that world with hard-won treasure. Jesus' disciples now incubate to ready themselves spiritually for clothing with power from on high. Richly clothed, they will then return to society to manifest God's presence.

Biblically, the incubatory stage is often just for an individual. It can be a solitary path, as Toynbee traces in the lives of St Paul, St Benedict and Dante. It was so for Moses in his sheep-tending years, an apparently unpromising time of exile. Moses surely experienced these years as ones of defeat, yet God was reshaping his character in preparation for encounter at a burning bush. In the upper room, though, this 'withdrawal' phase is communal. Against potential fragility, the disciples bond further, grounded in mutual support. The angels at the ascension have anchored them in this, effectively counselling them, 'Do not stand gazing in amazement. Weigh what you have heard. Go back to Scripture. Ready yourself for what has been promised.' This message both prepares the disciples for receiving the Spirit and unites them in inner work, just before the breaking of spiritual waters and the birthing of the early church.

The presence of women in the upper room reinforces this communality.[7] While the male disciples alone enjoyed the Last Supper in the upper room, the post-ascension community widens. Luke tells us that the disciples join in prayer 'along with the women' (Acts 1:14), Jesus' mother Mary and his brothers. This represents a paradigm shift. Historically, men and women worshipped in the temple separated by a wall. In the synagogue, they worshipped separated by a screen. Even today women and men pray in different, partitioned, areas before Jerusalem's Wailing Wall. In the upper room no wall divides them. Moreover, Luke tells us similarly that on the day of Pentecost, they are 'all together in one place' (Acts 2:1). Peter confirms this in his Pentecost sermon, quoting Joel who speaks of the outpouring of the Holy Spirit on 'all people', 'your sons and daughters' (Acts 2:17), and 'both men and women' (2:18). In this sermon, which converts three thousand people, Peter's quoting of Old Testament Scripture perfectly mirrors what the crowd has just witnessed. There is no contradiction. The Spirit has filled both women and men. Hudson Taylor, who employed female evangelists as part of his pioneering missionary work in China, comments: 'At Pentecost, God did not arrange a special women's meeting.'[8]

The faith, fidelity and empathy that the women have shown since Gethsemane suffuse the upper room during these ten days. This speaks of the feminine yearning and devotion required in any genuine longing for the Holy Spirit. No simple appeal for power will suffice. As Christian women like Maria Woodworth-Etter, Carrie Judd Montgomery, Aimee Semple McPherson, Kathryn Kuhlman and Heidi Baker have demonstrated, it is often depth of feminine longing and surrender that releases powerful Holy Spirit anointing. Such longing and surrender are equally available to men and women. However, they require mature psychological wholeness in men, as well as an appreciation for the distinctive role of women in God's economy.

The post-ascension phase brings together both sexes in close proximity. As Victor Turner, an expert on ritual process, observes, 'shared liminality' is essential for the formation of deep community.[9] 'Communitas', as Turner calls it, comes through shared burdens and trials. It is what emerges in natural disasters, even on a minor level for my family when floodwaters periodically invade our Oxford neighbourhood. Neighbours who have ignored each other for years suddenly compare damage, laugh with 'Blitz spirit', all social restraint dissolved. Leonard Hjalmarson discusses how formative community can emerge in the lives of people with urgent mutual needs:

> Communitas in a spiritual sense does not come from manufactured celebrations or events. Attending lots of meetings won't do it. Even parties and prayer meetings won't cut it. They depend on artificial stimulants of food, drink, music, shared common space and energy: lovely and probably necessary, but not transforming. True communitas comes from having walked through liminality together – and coming out the other side – forever different. It happens in AA groups all the time.[10]

Corporate change processes require protected spaces in which cries of the heart can be shared and new identities tested. In such liminal spaces, we share each other's needs and see our own in fresh perspective. Our spiritual development will always be personal and a journey that, in one sense, we take existentially alone. In another way, though, it is a corporate story. We go on together.

How I wished I'd known this truth of human formation in my pre-Christian years when I was spiritually lost. I tried therapy, I tried self-reflection, I tried meditation. Nothing, though, assists healing like the transforming power of shared liminal space. My initial surrender to Jesus as Lord was, of course, the turning point. But equally vital to my early Christian formation were the subsequent months I spent in an early morning men's group. Each Friday morning at 6.30 am, a close band of recent converts and wise elders would meet to confess their sins, disciple each other and gird each other up in prayer. This time of authenticity and vulnerability was equally heartily matched by time spent afterwards in a greasy-spoon cafe refuelling over a prodigiously ample cooked breakfast.

For the disciples, too, liminal formation emerges not just through close community but through corporate prayer. Spurgeon recommends such prayer gatherings, noting that 'You get warmed up by getting near to each other in your prayers'.[11] When the prayer temperature rises, we experience spiritual breakthrough and personal renewal. This is invigorating and strengthening at both individual and kingdom levels:

> When first one, and then another, and yet another, throws his whole soul into the prayer, the kingdom of heaven is conquered and the victory becomes great, indeed! . . . It is in the spirit of prayer that our strength lies! And if we lose this, the locks will be shorn from Samson and the Church of God will become weak as water.[12]

Corporate prayer prevails in any revival. It was so on the Hebridean island of Lewis, prior to the breakout of revival in 1949. An islander, Margaret MacLeod, testifies to her social circle having been 'a community at prayer'.[13] Many people attended Sunday services but attendance at the midweek prayer meeting defined church membership. For the disciples, the upper room is a prayer room in which they can petition, invoke and call down the Holy Spirit from heaven. This is not so much 'time out' as 'time in', during which they worship and pray. Whereas our culture tends either to be strung out at work or cloistered in the privacy of a therapy room, the upper room is both liminal space *and* outward-facing prayer command centre. Temporarily 'withdrawn' from the world, the disciples petition the Holy Spirit for his coming and their own 'return'.

According to Luke, the disciples praise God exultantly in the temple and join together constantly in the upper room in prayer. In Hungry, our monthly prayer meeting at St Aldates, our method is to worship at length before praying out of the overflow of God's presence. The disciples praise God, affirm his holiness and pray the Scriptures, especially those concerning the Holy Spirit's coming. Peter's quoting of Joel's prophecy in Acts 2 suggests that this Scripture has recently been on his lips. The ten-day meeting too will be a catalyst to many further prayer meetings in Acts. After the dearth of prayer meetings since Gethsemane, the disciples continually petition. It is as if awareness of Jesus interceding at his Father's side releases in them a new spirit of prayer.

For Ronald Rolheiser, the upper room prayer meeting underlines the value of our own church meetings.[14] When we tire of them, he reminds us that Pentecost came at such a gathering. In meetings, we wait for God to do something in and through us that we cannot do by ourselves: become a community at peace able to bring shalom and blessing to a hurting world. Spurgeon similarly underlines the fivefold apostolic purpose of the prayer meeting. For him, it is (1) 'to encourage a discouraged people', and to be (2) 'a place for the reception of divine power', (3) 'the resource of a persecuted Church', (4) 'a means of individual deliverance' and (5) 'the missionary's lever'.[15] Spurgeon then laconically itemizes hindrances to prayer meetings: unholiness, discord, hypocrisy, long prayers, lack of earnestness and absence of persevering follow-up effort. Functionally, the ten-day prayer meeting certainly fulfils his criteria of apostolic purposes. What constitutes the content of the disciples' prayers remains more of a mystery.

However, given how strategic prayer is to this discipleship phase, let me outline some vital premises of revival prayer. This is not to draw a simplistic equation between prayer methods and moves of God's Spirit. Spiritual outpouring always remains the sovereign prerogative of God. It is just to point to the correspondence between patterns of prayer and God's activity in history, and to posit what prayer principles may have been active in the upper room. As a prelude, we need to conform ourselves to a receptive shape in readiness to receive the gift of God's presence. We also need to live in expectation that God delights to pour out his grace at times and in places of his choosing. We can then progress to more specific principles that appear to underlie effective corporate prayer.

Deep prayer begins with a breaking up of the hard ground within. In Hosea 10:12, the prophet declares:

> Sow for yourselves righteousness,
>   reap the fruit of unfailing love,
> and break up your unploughed ground.

This 'unploughed ground' is the ground of our own heart. Intercessory prayer always involves self-examination and inner labour. Although we all resist vulnerability, Psalm 51:17 counsels:

> The sacrifices of God are a broken spirit;
>   a broken and contrite heart,
> O God, you will not despise.

Two places we must travel to in prayer are repentance and confession. The etymology of the Hebrew word for 'contrite' is 'bruised' or 'broken to pieces'. In prayer, we break up the ground and soften our heart. This surely describes the tenderizing process that the disciples must have begun after the events of the last forty days. Revival prayer begins in this place of self-honesty and tenderness of soul.

An intercessor also submits to a burden. Our culture begets individualism and self-focus, but intercessory prayer rejects this bias. Instead, we identify compassionately with others' needs. Charles Finney, the revivalist, defined prayer as a 'state of the heart', a quality not to be cultivated by any strategy but one arising from within:

> What constitutes a spirit of prayer? Is it many prayers and warm words? No. Prayer is the state of the heart. The spirit of prayer is a state of continual desire and anxiety of mind for the salvation of sinners . . . A Christian who has this spirit of prayer feels anxious for souls.[16]

This is a kind of unchecked empathy, where we feel another's burden as our own. We've had the metaphor of prayer as breaking. This is prayer as burden.

William Booth, in his famous *Vision of the Lost*, evokes this dimension of prayer. With powers of apocalyptic description, he portrays a tumult of wretched human beings sinking in a stormy ocean. He then describes others who have rescued themselves by climbing onto a towering rock. This crowd proceeds to pray that Jesus will come to them to gratify them, eliminate doubt, or provide reassurance that they will never again slip into the turbulent sea. The light is dawning for the reader. The crowd is Booth's acidic metaphor for the church. His allegory describes the tendency of the saved to become self-preoccupied, caught up in religion, rather than burdened for the lost souls still struggling in the waters. Finally, Booth pinpoints the figure of Jesus in this scene:

> These people used to meet and get up as high on the rock as they could, and looking towards the mainland (where they thought the Great Being was) they would cry out, 'Come to us! Come and help us!' And all the while He was down (by His Spirit) among the poor struggling, drowning creatures in the angry deep, with His arms around them trying to drag them out, and looking up – oh! so longingly but all in vain – to those on the rock, crying to them with His voice all hoarse from calling, 'Come to Me! Come, and help Me!'[17]

Jesus does not stand detached on some spiritual mainland. He struggles in the perilous waters, desperate to reach the unsaved. The church's efforts and prayers should be aligned with his burdened heart. It is not enough for our hearts to be contrite, important though personal mortification may be. They must also be burdened for others' plight. We can preoccupy ourselves with the mechanics of prayer but, if our fundamental heart orientation is faulty, Booth's vision implies, we will never pray what Jesus is praying. We will be lost in an echo chamber of our making.

Our heart breaks and is burdened. However, do we pray with right motives? The third dimension of prayer, after confession and embracing burden, involves fierce heart interrogation. The psalmist monitors the inner leanings of his heart, stressing the need for absolute integrity in prayer:

> Hear, O LORD, my righteous plea;
> listen to my cry.
> Give ear to my prayer –
> it does not rise from deceitful lips.
> (Psalm 17:1)

Similarly in Psalm 66:18, the psalmist acknowledges, 'If I had cherished sin in my heart, the Lord would not have listened.' Ruthless self-interrogation marked revival prayer meetings on Lewis in 1949. Duncan Campbell records one night when the fierce self-inquiry of a youth, Kenneth MacDonald, precipitated a move of the Holy Spirit:

> One young man took up his Bible and read from Psalm 24: 'Who shall stand in His holy place? He that hath clean hands and a pure heart . . . He shall receive the blessing from the Lord.' The young man closed the Bible and, looking at his companions on their knees before God, he cried: 'Brethren, it is just so much humbug to be waiting thus night after night, month after month, if we ourselves are not right with God. I must ask myself – "Is my heart pure? Are my hands clean?"'[18]

It was MacDonald's own right standing with God, freely offered for God's evaluation, that, in the next moment, led to the Holy Spirit descending in a flood on the gathering. MacDonald was offering himself for divine examination before others. Will we? We need to examine our core motives in prayer. Why do we pray for an outpouring of the Holy Spirit? Why do we pray for revival? Really?

Broken of heart, burdened for others, praying with right motive, our prayers will necessarily be full of passion. Our culture exalts remaining cool and disengaged, but for the Christian passionate engagement leads to fullness of life. The cry of revival prayers is often prefaced by an 'Oh' of passionate exclamation, as in:

> Oh, that you would rend the heavens and come down,
> that the mountains would tremble before you!
> (Isaiah 64:1)

Jesus himself offers up prayers to his Father with loud cries and tears. Jacob wrestles with God in prayer. The diaries of saints are full of imagery of wrestling, sweating and bleeding in prayer's passionate pursuit. David Brainerd's account of his prayer life among the native American Indians in the 1740s is almost shocking in its intensity. Reviewing the Lewis church's prayer culture in the 1949 revival, two authors conclude: 'The gospel of a broken heart demands the ministry of bleeding hearts. True intercession is sacrifice. When we cease to bleed, we cease to bless.'[19] We may recoil from this intensity or feel ashamed of our own half-hearted cries. But, like so much else in the life of faith, this is an invitation to engage further in the spiritual gymnasium of prayer. Just as our physical muscles atrophy when unused, so our prayer muscles wither if we are not regularly engaged in intercession. We can grow in our capacity to stand in the gap and passionately intercede for others, but we will need to exercise regularly to be effective in this pursuit. Self-examination is again vital. To what degree are we invested in our praying? Is our object of prayer a matter of personal passion? Or is our heart secretly distant? Let us follow Jesus who was not afraid to cry out to God, weep tears of distress and sweat blood in pursuit of his inmost longings.

Praying passionately, our praying not only petitions God but it becomes a vehicle for our personal transformation. It begins to reshape us. As C. S. Lewis said, prayer doesn't change God so much as it changes us. As we come into God's presence in prayer, the Holy Spirit convicts us of personal impurity. Praying for God's outpouring goes hand in hand with growth in holiness. Both aspects underlie one of the great revival prayer texts from Isaiah, which believers constantly pleaded in the run-up to the Lewis Awakening:

> Then will the eyes of the blind be opened
>   and the ears of the deaf unstopped.
> Then will the lame leap like a deer,
>   and the mute tongue shout for joy.
> Water will gush forth in the wilderness
>   and streams in the desert . . .
> And a highway will be there;
>   it will be called the Way of Holiness.
> (Isaiah 35:5–6, 8)

Every one of our prayers can potentially drive a new stake of personal repentance into the ground. The Victorian evangelist Gypsy Smith counselled those longing for revival to draw a chalk circle around them and to ask God to start a revival within this circle. Corporate revival always begins with personal renewal.

Kenneth MacDonald interrogated his own probity and his prayer colleagues' purity. After his question, 'O God, are my hands clean? Is my heart pure?', report tells us:

> At that moment the presence of God flooded the place and several of the men fainted or fell into a trance, with the overwhelming awareness of the Eternal. God had come to them

> in this wonderful and humbling manifestation. John Smith said that at that moment they all became aware that the holiness of God and revival were inextricably linked. God came, and when He came, it was in a revelation of his holiness.[20]

As the disciples pray in the upper room, they walk further along the highway of holiness. They enter a deeper understanding of God's holiness and are further sanctified. Perhaps at last they can say that their hands too are clean, their hearts too are pure.

We must also pray the promises of God in trust that he will fulfil them in our lives. In one sense, this should have been my first premise of prayer. A theology of God as covenant-keeper is foundational to prayer: meaningful communication with a God who has proclaimed his covenant promises and who vows to see them fulfilled in his children's lives. In practice, though, we cannot demand that God fulfil his promises unless we are contritely engaged with him first. We need to have poured out our prayers with sincerity and right motive before we are worthy of addressing God in this way.

This represents a vital graduation in our prayer lives. As Duncan Campbell said, 'Desire for revival is one thing; confident anticipation that our desire will be fulfilled is another.'[21] We can enjoy this confidence because we see God's Scriptural promises fulfilled in history. We also know many fulfilled in our lives. As we progress in prayer, we grow in conviction of God's fidelity to his promises. A chronicler of the Lewis revival describes how in one prayer meeting, a blacksmith ended his prayers with a challenge to his Maker:

> 'God, do you not know that your honour is at stake? You promised to pour floods on dry ground, and you are not doing it.' He paused for a while and then concluded: 'God, your honour is

> at stake, and I challenge you to keep your covenant engagements.' Duncan Campbell recalls at that moment, 'That whole granite house shook like a leaf', and whilst one elder thought of an earth tremor, Duncan was reminded of Acts 4:31: 'After they prayed, the place where they were meeting was shaken . . .' Duncan Campbell pronounced the benediction and they went outside. It was about two o'clock in the morning and they found 'the whole village alive, ablaze with God'. Men and women were carrying chairs and asking if there was room in the church for them![22]

In Luke 24:49, Jesus vows to send what his Father has promised: the Holy Spirit. In the upper room, the disciples prayerfully stand on this double promise. It will be because of this that Peter can so persuasively explain at Pentecost that the disciples are not drunk but filled with the Spirit. Peter will confirm Joel's prophecy with his own prophetic verification, 'This is that!' The disciples have established this ground in the preceding ten days. Confident of their right standing and claiming God's promises, they have prayed, as we need to: 'Lord, as I have been resolute praying for this outpouring with all my heart, will you now be resolute in keeping your covenant engagements?'

Our culture craves immediate solutions. By contrast, Karl Barth asserts: 'Only where the Spirit is sighed, cried and prayed for does he become present and newly active.'[23] This points to the utmost need for perseverance in prayer. Etymologically, the word 'Paraclete' means 'the one who answers a call'. The disciples' prayers are steeped in a spirit of perseverance. They follow the watchmen in Isaiah who petition God day and night, giving him no peace:

> I have posted watchmen on your walls, O Jerusalem;
> they will never be silent day or night.

> You who call on the LORD,
> give yourselves no rest.
> (Isaiah 62:6)

In Revelation 5, St John draws back a theatrical curtain to reveal a vision of four living creatures and elders in heaven's throne room, bowed down before the Lamb. They hold golden bowls full of incense, 'which are the prayers of the saints' (5:8). Our prayers are stored up in bowls, then, held aloft before God. The image is one of progressive accumulation rather than immediate call and response. Much as we seek instant gratification, it is often only when we pray to breaking, exhaust ourselves and confront our weakness that we experience divine breakthrough. Ernest Baker, in his intensive study of the revivals in the Bible, underlines this importance of perseverance in prayer:

> God's best things can only be given to those who show appreciation of their value by persistent desire and effort to obtain them . . . The prayers which reveal the settled longing of the heart are the prayers He heeds. And it takes time to reveal that such desires are possessed by us.[24]

The steadfast heart prays persistently. It works with repeated action to erode a rock, rather than naively assuming the impact of a sudden hammer blow. We may pray, unanswered for weeks, months or even years, and then a single prayer will occasion the collapse of a progressively weakened spiritual stronghold. Although we would like to condense the gap between passionate prayer and divine response, God's timeline is not ours, calibrated as it is according to eternity. Certain of our prayers in this age may only be answered in the next. We therefore pray in trust, restless and impatient for answers in our youth, and often more patient and philosophical in maturity.

Often before revivals break forth, steady pressure of prayer intensifies in a community's life. Thus it was in the 1859 Ulster revival. Months previously, James McQuilkin and four friends had started meeting weekly for Bible study and prayer. Their heartfelt cry was 'for an outpouring of the Holy Spirit upon ourselves and upon the surrounding country. This was the one great object and burden of our prayers. We held right to the one thing and did not run off to anything else'; the local populace ridiculed this prayer group, 'but we kept right on praying until the power came'.[25] When it did, a hundred thousand Ulster men and women came to faith in the following year. Carried through persistence to bolder levels of appeal, the five friends saw their inmost aspirations fulfilled. This begs questions of our prayer lives. Will we keep on praying until the power comes? However much ridicule we meet? Will we hold right to the one thing and not run off to anything else?

Finally, we come to the motif of 'begging', one central to a developed understanding of prayer. This begging is not about craven submission before a fierce, demanding God. It is about a self-shaping of the kind that cultural critic Lewis Hyde describes of creative people:

> An essential portion of the artist's labour is not creation so much as invocation. Part of the work cannot be made, it must be received; we cannot have this gift except, perhaps, by supplication, by courting, by creating within ourselves that 'begging bowl' to which the gift is drawn.[26]

Hyde's dynamic significantly pertains to prayer and any significant shift of life direction. Shortly before coming to faith,

I sought to transition from working as a theatre director to taking up a junior role in a documentary company. This period represented the end of a long-cherished dream in theatre and occasioned much personal grief. The reason that I endured such cost was to shape a securer life and support a potential future wife and family. Holding my desired end in mind, I worked to reverse-engineer my situation to live towards that goal. I conformed myself to a certain shape, reaching out for a future destiny. This involved changing priorities, self-denial and the sacrifice of a beloved vocation. Most of all, it involved trust until that potential wife appeared on the scene. I had to create within myself a begging bowl to which the gift would be drawn.

This work of emptying out is intrinsic to prayer. Prayer begins with adoration of God and acknowledgment of our emptiness – 'Lord, help me with this thing I need.' Before being clothed with power from on high, the disciples need to recognize their spiritual poverty. In prayer, they need to buy from God golden wisdom refined in fire, white clothes of forgiveness to cover their shameful sinfulness, and eye-salve to see (Revelation 3:17–18). As they offer themselves as these begging bowls, God then fills them. A. J. Gordon, the American Baptist preacher, describes this spiritual dynamic:

> We know that the wind lusteth to blow where there is a vacuum . . . If we could expel all pride, vanity, self-righteousness, self-seeking, desire for applause, honor and promotion, – if by some divine power we should be utterly emptied of all that, – the Spirit would come as rushing mighty wind to fill us.[27]

Every saint who has experienced a baptism in the Holy Spirit testifies to this pattern. Only emptied of everything not of God can we be filled with him; and this emptying, so anathema to the contrarian human heart, comes as a result of our spiritual hunger:

> First, there is the hunger of heart, often followed by a sense of desperation that leads to utter surrender of self. Thereafter there is the meeting of the soul with God in whatever manner the Almighty is pleased to reveal Himself to the desperate seeker who, like Jacob at Jabbok, will not let Him go until there is blessing.[28]

The disciples arrive at this point following the ascension. Hunger of heart, surrender of self and prayerful wrestling converge. This is the difference between revival and 'business as normal' church. As Charles Finney said of the Chicago Revival of 1857–8:

> There is such a general confidence in the prevalence of prayer that the people very extensively seemed to prefer meeting for prayer to meeting for preaching. The general impression seemed to be, 'We have had instruction until we are hardened; it is time for us to pray.'[29]

In our own times, Leonard Ravenhill has castigated the church for privileging preaching over intercession, exhorting us to embrace the simplicity, humility and spirituality of prayer. While un-anointed preaching by pastors can harden us, anointed praying softens our heart and makes us permeable to God's purposes.

At this chapter's end, therefore, I want to leave you with a question. Do you spend time in your own upper room, praying to be clothed with power from on high? Will you make it your ambition to pray for a new outpouring of the Holy Spirit? Will you pray with others? Will you pray even if you are in a minority of one? The Holy Spirit will pour himself out afresh but only if we call on him with passion. We can each begin right now by inserting our name in this prayer of Habbakuk (3:2), making a classic revival prayer our own:

> Lord, I [*insert your name*] have heard of your fame;
> I [*insert your name*] stand in awe of your deeds, O Lord.
> Renew them in our day,
> in our time make them known.

'Christianity is incendiarism; Christianity is fire setting;
a Christian is a person set on fire.'
Søren Kierkegaard[1]

'The supreme need of the Church is the same in the
twentieth century as in the first – it is men on fire for Christ.
I beg you do not commit the fearful blunder
of dampening down that flame.'
James Stuart Stewart[2]

9

Filled

'Suppose we try Pentecost?' asked Samuel Chadwick, the early twentieth-century Methodist preacher and teacher.[3] He was considering the desperate need for a revitalized church. Chadwick's laconic question is a reminder that personal Pentecost has not always been of high value for the church. By contrast, the coming of the Holy Spirit at Pentecost changes everything, fulfilling Old Testament prophecy that speaks of an outpouring of God's Spirit on all people. The disciples' fifty-day transitioning is over. However, the disciples require more than natural gifts for the platform on which they will minister. They need God's empowering presence. Knowing this, they have assiduously sought God's filling and the clothing of power in prayer.

Hudson Taylor berates a post-Pentecost church too often consumed with method, machinery and resources; instead he urges on it ten days of waiting prayer in order to seek 'the source of power'.[4] How often as disciples do we personally or corporately suspend our activity until we experience breakthrough with God? Such prayerful focus, when devotedly pursued, always yields great fruit. In the history of St Aldates, I think of the year 1993 when Rector David MacInnes felt led by God to lay down the ministries of the church and wait in prayer for God's new leading. The result was a dramatic manifestation of the Holy Spirit in meetings. In this season, the church leadership had been considering a significant spatial reordering of the church. Yet, as David MacInnes has said, it seemed God intended that a reordering of the congregation take place first. This time of prayerful waiting was not easy for many. They would have preferred to continue the church's activist programme. However, this was a seminal time of ministry by the Holy Spirit, which resulted in confession of sin, healing and deliverance. It paved the way for cleansing and fresh vision for our church.

The post-ascension community has waited patiently in prayer. Next, like much that is a sovereign move of God, the Holy Spirit's coming is sudden and unexpected. Drawing on Lewis Hyde's observation about creativity, part of the spiritual work in which we are engaged 'cannot be made, it must be received'.[5] Pentecost marks the moment in which God pours his Spirit into the begging bowl into which we have shaped ourselves. His Spirit arrives not into the outstretched hands of a beggar but the body and being of a surrendered soul. It is a moment of pure gift, in which God indwells us.

Ronald Rolheiser describes this as receiving the Spirit in order to live the resurrected life that we are already living.[6] This is true, although Rolheiser does not explain this process in charismatic terms; indeed in my view, he over-psychologizes a process that Scripture describes as entirely supernatural. The Bible itself provides myriad supernatural images to describe the Spirit's coming to live within us. These range from the gentle alighting of a dove to a mighty shaking by wind and fire. Given these metaphors, psychology alone will never fully answer what this inrush of life involves. While the non-believer may understand some psychological correlative for dying and rising, it is impossible to articulate the Spirit's reception properly except in transcendent terms. This is not some holiday moment of infusion and feeling vitally alive. It is an unmediated encounter with the living God. It marks a person's profound experience of the reality of God's presence.

Scripturally, Pentecost is a moment of pure deluge, akin to the experience of standing beneath a cascading waterfall. Having had recent experience of this in a jungle clearing, I can testify not only to the revivifying presence of crashing water but the hammering impact of a funnelled blow of water descending on one's head. Pentecost is an open heaven event in which God's power infuses the disciples' beings. For these reasons, it can provoke anxiety, especially in the buttoned-up English soul. I have seen people touched tremendously quietly over time by the Spirit's presence, also seen them shake or prostrate beneath the weight of God's glory. A personal Pentecost, though, always follows a series of inward shifts in a person's being. Two spiritual directors write of it as a threshold where 'the interior forces of convergence become so strong and concentrated that they produce a breakthrough, a new and improved mode of being'.[7] Their example of this process is the convulsive birth of the USA in 1776 out of the thirteen founding colonies.

Improbable as it may seem, Pentecost is thus both earthquake and harvest, the final razing of what has been and a late summer gathering of fruit. Earthquakes and harvests are products of innumerable former processes converging in a single moment. An earthquake is the concentrated product of the invisible shifting of tectonic plates. This moment of grand buckling in the earth's crust is matched by other extreme weather phenomena, each necessitating new responses from those caught in their midst. As a writer on the 1998 American East Coast ice storm reported, 'Power seemed to be out across the village. I was alive – it was as if the power left the grid and poured into me.'[8] At Pentecost, power leaves God's grid and infuses us. Similarly, a spiritual harvest, like an agricultural one, is the culmination of a season of sowing and labouring. In fitting recognition of this, Pentecost takes place at the time of the Jewish harvest festival of that name.

Even earthquake and harvest metaphors, though, fail to capture the thrillingly personal nature of this encounter. For that we must listen to a man like Samuel Logan Brengle (1860–1936), future preacher, teacher and Commissioner for the Salvation Army. He awoke one morning with an overwhelming desire for personal holiness:

> Getting out of bed about six o'clock with that desire, I opened my Bible and, while reading some of the words of Jesus, He gave me such a blessing as I never had dreamed a man could have this side of heaven. It was an unutterable revelation. It was a heaven of love that came into my heart. My soul melted like wax before fire. I sobbed and sobbed. I loathed myself that I had ever sinned against Him or doubted Him or lived for myself and not for His glory. Every ambition for self was now gone. The pure flame of love burned it like a blazing fire would burn a moth.[9]

With his language of melting, blazing and burning, Brengle echoes biblical accounts of the Holy Spirit as fire. He points to the purifying, refining nature of this encounter. Moreover, he experiences both 'a heaven of love' and an aching hunger for holiness and sacrificial service. The Spirit's empowering is never for our personal convenience. Rather, his propulsive power releases the believer into selfless serving. This is a crucible experience, intense, almost overpowering, but with cleansing and refining purpose. It testifies, above all, to God's tremendous love for us and his concern for our right standing before him. For Brengle, life was never the same again.

Another man transformed by his Holy Spirit encounter was the Bradford plumber turned evangelist and healer, Smith Wigglesworth. His experience, like that of many, including baptized believers in the book of Acts, was of a further filling of the Spirit subsequent to his conversion. Theologically, the Spirit comes to live in us at our conversion, but the book of Acts and church history describe the additional possibility of infilling experiences prior to or following this event. For Wigglesworth, it occurred post-conversion in the living room of a Sunderland vicarage, after a vicar's wife, Mrs Boddy, laid hands upon him. Wigglesworth had travelled to the area following reports of revival to attend a conference led by the Reverend Alexander Boddy. In that living room, as Wigglesworth complained of not having received the gift of tongues at the conference, Mrs Boddy replied tartly that it was not tongues but 'the Baptism' that he required.[10] Praying for him, she left the room to answer a visitor. Wigglesworth reports:

> The fire fell. It was a wonderful time as I was there with God alone. He bathed me in power. I was conscious of the cleansing of the precious Blood, and I cried out: 'Clean! Clean! Clean!' I was filled with the joy of the consciousness of the cleansing. I was given a vision in which I saw the Lord Jesus Christ. I beheld the empty cross, and I saw Him exalted at the right hand of God the Father. I could speak no longer in English but I began to praise Him in other tongues as the Spirit of God gave me utterance. I knew then, although I might have received anointings previously, that

> now, at last, I had received the real Baptism in the Holy Spirit as they received on the day of Pentecost.[11]

Wigglesworth's imagery mixes falling fire and baptismal cleansing waters. There is both sharp purging and invigorating joy. His description recalls Eustace's 'un-dragoning' in *The Voyage of the Dawn Treader* by C. S. Lewis, an experience of both bracing pain and delicious healing, as when we tear a hardened scab from the new skin beneath.[12]

Finally, Wigglesworth experiences an epiphany, a vision of the vacant cross with Christ exalted at his Father's side. Thus, the Holy Spirit comes not to draw focus but to point away from himself to Christ's sacrifice and ascended glory. The theologian Tom Smail made this discovery when he dared to speak in tongues for the first time in public at a Pentecostal conference. A young woman gave him the interpretation: 'There is no way to Pentecost except by Calvary; the Spirit is given from the cross.'[13]

Pentecost represents a watershed in the disciples' lives. For the last fifty days, they may have wrestled with restless scepticism (Thomas) or corrosive guilt (Peter). Now the experience of being drenched with the Holy Spirit collectively transforms them. From fugitives skulking in locked rooms, they burst on to the public stage, proclaiming their faith. Peter graduates into an anointed preacher, his words of power precipitating three thousand conversions. Neither of his encounters with the incarnate or risen Jesus involved such infusing and unction. In my life, I remember a middle-aged English housekeeper whom I met in the south of France. Chopping vegetables in her kitchen, she recounted her recent coming to faith, how she had been drinking hard through unhappiness, only to find herself one day, to her surprise, watching a Christian TV channel as Joyce Meyer preached.

Within minutes, the Holy Spirit had fallen on her, pressing her to the floor. Here she lay prostrate for hours. On those kitchen tiles, washed by the Spirit and knowing the Father's great love, she gave her life to Christ.

My own experience shifts us from a sun-drenched kitchen in southern France to a damp basement in a salt-stained Eastbourne hotel. It was here that personal unhappiness led me in 2002. For some years, besides labouring with depression, I had battled with split-second violent thoughts towards passers-by in the street. Psychologists would term these 'intrusive thoughts', which many of us know as part of the flotsam and jetsam of our mental lives. However, I knew my momentary thoughts of violent intent were not psychological in origin, beginning as they had after a fit of explosive anger during a relationship breakdown. For some years, as a non-Christian, I had taken these thoughts to the therapy room, despite protesting to one therapist, 'I feel that what I really need is an exorcist.' 'Don't worry,' she replied, 'it's just a neurosis, we'll get to the bottom of it.' Get to the bottom of it we never did. For, as I intuited, those impulses had a spiritual root and required a spiritual solution. That came one day in that hotel basement as a worship leader prayed for me, his hand pressed against my stomach. Would I have preferred a more discreet remedy applied in the privacy of a therapy room? Of course. God's solution came as part of my awkward attendance at an Alpha Holy Spirit weekend. New Testament healing is invariably corporate. As a psychologically literate person, this exposure was embarrassing. I cannot deny, though, what this prayer precipitated: a flushing and total expunging of darkness from my being. As prayer expelled the source of these violent thoughts, a cloud bank of depression lifted from me. Helpful though it was, what three years of therapy had not dislodged in this regard was gone in fifteen minutes.

Then, after healing, came infusion. Within minutes, the church leader prayed for the Holy Spirit to fill the dark places in me that had been vacated. God's love flooded in. As Pascal wrote of his midnight experience of filling by the Holy Spirit, 'Joy, Joy, Joy, tears of Joy'.[14] I don't know how long I remained with my arms uplifted in worship and praise. I only remember that I never wanted it to stop. It was too glorious resting in God's presence. Was this the end of 'neurosis'? No, it was something far deeper than that. How can I 'prove' it? I can't. But I know what I know what I know.

For me, as for many, Pentecost involved drama, surrender, the experience of being intimately known and a personal homecoming. Pentecost need not, however, be so dramatic or the preserve of the mystically inclined. It has often been otherwise, even with heroes of the faith. What it is always, though, is transformative. Witness Oswald Chambers, a man prodigiously used by God. Of his own filling, he recorded, 'I had no vision of heaven or of angels, I had nothing. I was as dry and empty as ever, no power or realization of God, no witness of the Holy Spirit.'[15] Yet Chambers knew something had happened. 'Then I was asked to speak at a meeting, and forty souls came out to the front. Did I praise God? No, I was terrified and left them to the workers.'[16]

This brilliantly honest account will greatly comfort many of us. Here Chambers confesses that his personal Pentecost was a drab affair, admitting astonishment at the sudden difference that it caused in his preaching, and then hilariously absenting himself in terrified flight from his new converts. This was the celebrated Christian hero who captivated a generation of soldiers based in Cairo in the First World War and who died leaving a harvest of writings that has sustained Christians for a century.

Brengle, Wigglesworth, Chambers – all witnessed a connection between their filling and their subsequent service for Christ. Spirit-empowerment is never about personal giddiness. It is, in the title of a book by Raniero Cantalamessa, preacher to the papal household, a 'sober intoxication of the Spirit'.[17] This is non-alcoholic, clear-headed joy. To understand further this connection between Spirit infilling and service, we must return to Douglas Brown, the Baptist minister whom we left arrested in his night-time study. We can ask to be filled by the Holy Spirit, as people do at the end of our Sunday services at St Aldates when we offer such an invitation. However, God can also commission us with a new calling for which further Spirit infilling is essential. Such was the case with Duncan Brown. He had received an invitation to preach in Folkestone as part of a week-long mission in early 1921, but God was also calling him to a wider evangelistic ministry beyond his church's walls. We have already read of the problem that this presented to his pride, evident in his infuriated riposte to God: 'I cannot get into the pulpit and plead with people. It is against my temperament.'[18]

Brown endured a four-month crisis from October 1920 to February 1921 before God over-ruled his will. Describing himself as Jacob grappling with the angel, Brown wrote, 'All through January God wrestled with me. There is a love that will not let us go. Glory be to God!'[19] In retrospect, he saw that God desired his greater blessing. At the time, though, as so often with us in our spiritual wrestling, he blamed his circumstances, remaining blind to his own spiritual failings. On a February night, only four days before departure for Lowestoft, Brown reached breaking point. While praying on his knees in his study at 2 am, his dog licked his face. Brown felt only loveless.

> Then something happened. I found myself in the loving embrace of Christ for ever and ever; and all power and joy and all

> blessedness rolled in like a deluge. How did it come? I cannot tell you. Perhaps I may when I get to heaven. All explanations are there, but the experience is here . . . God had waited four months for a man like me; and I said, 'Lord Jesus, I know what you want; You want me to go into mission work. I love thee more than I dislike that.' I did not hear any rustling of angels' wings. I did not see any sudden light.[20]

As with Chambers, what a bracingly candid account. In this testimony, Brown identifies many of the obstacles blocking us from receiving more of God's Spirit: a recoiling from a new calling on our life, a pleading of our personality and lack of abilities (one thinks of Moses at the burning bush), and a stubborn focus on the apparent horror of the call rather than on the glory of loving Jesus. Then Brown experiences an epiphany of love, power and joy. Yet even when he agrees to his commission, he notes that he does not hear any rustling of angels' wings or experience any confirmatory explosion of light.

We need more such accounts of the spiritual lives of believers. Brown's honesty will resonate with many in an age like ours that prizes personal authenticity and where charismatic experience is often hyped. At the same time, God brooks no resistance to his pre-ordained plan. For months, like Jonah fleeing God's call, Brown had wrestled in the belly of the beast. Finally, he could not deny God's calling on his life. The minister encountered a new dimension to God's love and yielded in exhausted assent.

Two thousand years earlier, God propelled the disciples into assenting action. The fruit of their first day of ministry was three thousand converts. The fruit of Brown's baptism of the Spirit was no less remarkable, given the faith-ravaged landscape of post-First World War Britain: five hundred conversions in the first five weeks of his Lowestoft mission. The Scottish preacher Duncan Campbell bore similar fruit in the Hebridean Revival of 1949–52, following his own turning point in ministry.

As with Brown, critical in Campbell's reformation was the realization of his ministerial pride. Is there an emerging message here for many of us in church leadership? Sitting on an Edinburgh convention platform, Campbell realized the poverty of his self-satisfaction at being booked to speak at five conventions that year. I have experienced something myself of this sudden consciousness of personal vanity about ministry achievement on hearing a preacher read out the ascended Jesus' words to the church in Laodicea: 'You say, "I am rich; I have acquired wealth and do not need a thing." But you do not realize that you are wretched, pitiful, poor, blind and naked' (Revelation 3:17–18). How easy it is to assume our spiritual wealth in denial of our actual poverty. How futile it is to assume God would pour his Spirit into such an unworthy vessel. By contrast, at the end of their fifty days, the apostles in the upper room have realized their beggarly status. They have emptied themselves through the disciplines of worship, prayer and fasting. They now crave gold refined in fire, the white clothes of the newly baptized and fresh, penetrating vision. God will bestow all of these liberally at Pentecost.

So it was with Duncan Campbell once he had, like Douglas Brown, reached breaking point. As with Brown, his night sea-journey culminated in his study and with surrender:

> That night in desperation on the floor of my study, I cast myself afresh on the mercy of God. He heard my cry for pardon and cleansing, and, as I lay prostrate before Him, wave after wave of Divine consciousness came over me, and the love of the Saviour flooded my being; and in that hour I knew that my life and

> ministry could never be the same again . . . If in any small measure God has been pleased to use me, it is all because of what He did for me that night.[21]

Until Campbell and Brown reached this point of no return, they were unable to receive God's blessing or fulfil his commission. Dying to self, rising to new life and receiving the Holy Spirit always involve loosening control, vulnerability, and willingness to change. When these men surrendered, their personal revivals became catalysts for dramatic revival in wider communities.

Remaining spiritually realistic, we must counterpoint these triumphant accounts of revival with the renunciations and sacrifices involved. In Campbell's case, he had to resign from leading his church, persuade the Faith Mission Council to employ a fifty-year-old man with a family, and leave home for an itinerant ministry in the Scottish islands. Epiphany may gain us access to the Promised Land, but we don't necessarily arrive there comfortable or garlanded in glory. So it is with the many refugees from war-torn lands currently streaming into Europe, with empty pockets and lacking the customary resources of home. In the words of poet David Whyte:

> It seems to be the nature of any new territory that we arrive on its borders flat broke. Any new world seems to demand dispossession and simplification. We look back in longing for our previous comforts, which, for all their smallness and poverty, at least had the richness of familiarity.[22]

In the face of the radical simplification involved in change, it is easy to retreat into our smaller concerns and remain wanderers, as the Israelites did for so long in the wilderness. Thankfully, Brown and Campbell knew true 'passing over' and deliverance from their previous confining obsessions. However, they both paid a cost in forsaking security and comfort and enduring exposure on a more dangerous stage, in knife-edge reliance on the Holy Spirit's provision. We can only remain thankful for their faith and courage. God's love had not let them go and, responding, they offered the source of living water to others. Campbell records in his Lewis campaign diary that at 3 am at a prayer meeting after his first evening of preaching, simply, 'GOD SWEPT IN'.[23] Testifying of the aftermath of his night of baptism, Brown wrote, 'Within four days I was in Lowestoft; the cloud burst, and souls were being born again by the score.'[24]

How do we receive the Holy Spirit? Samuel Chadwick urges four things of his readers: Repent, Ask, Receive and Obey.[25] A. W. Tozer, in his own four-point list, counsels: Surrender, Ask, Obey and Believe.[26] We might supplement their lists with Jesus' 'Wait' to his disciples: 'Do not leave Jerusalem, but wait for the gift my Father promised' (Acts 1:4). Geographically waiting in Jerusalem is key; metaphorically, we might say remaining intimately close to God's presence, not taking flight via the road to Emmaus. For an image to meditate on, we might return to the begging bowl, with its implications for personal emptying, cleansing and patient waiting for donation.

Repentance was my personal doorway to receiving the Holy Spirit. Prior to ministry time in that Eastbourne basement, sitting across a coffee table from a young woman, my need for spiritual 'un-dragoning' became apparent. Unexpectedly, I experienced the intrusive violent thought that had bedevilled me for six years. Fleeing to my hotel bedroom, I threw myself on my knees, with tears streaming down my face. My prayer was: 'Lord, I am so glad that I know you now. But I don't know what these thoughts are in me. Lord, I beg you, take them away from me. I turn away from tolerating these thoughts any longer. I hate them. Take them away or I will die.' Rarely have I known such a penetrating hatred of sin. It was this 'metanoia' that precipitated my deliverance and my subsequent reception of the Holy Spirit in that basement.

Today, it can become a meme of our charismatic services to offer an invitation to be clothed with power from on high. Tozer condemns the desire for 'the thrill or the victory or the power' implied.[27] Biblically, being filled with the Spirit is a discipleship threshold and, in its most radical form, is always the fruit of preparation. It leads to new eyes for our fellow human beings. Now, in Chambers' words:

> When you see men and women who should be princes and princesses with God bound up by the show of things – oh, you begin to understand what the Apostle meant when he said he wished himself accursed from Christ that men might be saved![28]

For the Spirit-filled believer, the challenge is then to continue in intimate, sensitive communion with the Spirit, lest we grieve him. St Aldates is a church that has known significant renewal through the Spirit in the last decades. How earnestly, though, we often pray, 'Lord, do not take your Holy Spirit from us' (Psalm 51:11). Many things can grieve the Holy Spirit: persistent sin in our lives, disunity with other churches, or a functional attitude where we prize the Spirit for what he can give us rather than for who he is. Those in whom the Spirit comes to live host God's presence. South African preacher Andrew Murray turned this reality into a meditative reflection: 'I am His Temple, and in the secret place He sits upon his throne.'[29] Following Pentecost, how the disciples must have been sensitive to their being living temples, having witnessed Christ's ascension and heard him speak of the coming gift of the Spirit. Murray turns his own meditation into a personal prayer that we can repeat as our own:

> I do now tremblingly accept the blessed truth: God the Spirit, the Holy Spirit, who is God Almighty dwells in me. O my Father, reveal within me what it means, lest I sin against Thee by saying it and not living it.[30]

What might it mean to grieve the Spirit? God once pictured this for me through a Japanese theatre production of *Macbeth*, enacted within Samurai culture. The entire action took place within a traditional Japanese household, framed by vast temple doors. Two elderly female temple attendants opened up these sliding doors to permit us to gaze inside. Here, the play's scenes, including snow-bound battles, unfolded. As the tragic hero Macbeth embarked on his road to ruin, violating every sacred norm, these two attendants sat rocking and keening on opposite sides of the stage. Functioning as spiritual witnesses, they lamented Macbeth's transgressions of conscience, community and creation. It was as if the Holy Spirit grieved for the sullying of everything glorious in Macbeth's being. Does the Holy Spirit grieve similarly in us? I believe so.

Wonderfully, if we sense his grieving, we can confess, receive God's forgiveness and know new awakening. A revival in Manchuria at the start of the twentieth century saw this occur at a corporate level. Jonathan Goforth, a Canadian Presbyterian missionary to China, was a man steeped in God's word (he read the Bible seventy-three times in his lifetime). Inspired by reading reports of the Welsh Revival across the globe, he had a revelation in his understanding of the Spirit and preached afresh on this topic from 1906 to 1908. Dr Murdock McKenzie, a phlegmatic Scot, wrote of the revival that followed at

Goforth's mission station at Changte, where many were convicted of their sin:

> That which weighed most heavily on the consciences of all was that we had so long been grieving the Holy Spirit by not giving Him His rightful place in our hearts and in our work. While believing in Him we had not trusted in Him, to work in and through us. Now we believe, we have learned our lesson that it is not by might, nor by power, but by my Spirit, saith the Lord of host (*sic*). May we never forget that lesson.[31]

Thankfully these believers fell on their knees afresh, experiencing incendiary revival as a result. How desperately the Church needs a new convicting by the Holy Spirit today. Where the Spirit has been grieved, will we allow him to tenderize our hearts and consciences again? How radically we might see transformation in our communities if we give him his rightful place again at the centre of our hearts and work.

Pentecost followed concentrated, corporate prayer. We need to embrace such prayer in an age of desperate spiritual need and contestation. For one prayerful heart cry to imitate, we can listen to Johann Christoph Blumhardt, a nineteenth-century Lutheran minister in Germany. Following a singular exorcism for which he prayed, Blumhardt witnessed the Holy Spirit sweep in power through the communities of the Black Forest. Believing in Pentecost at the level not just of personal salvation but of corporate healing and socio-political renewal, Blumhardt hungered for the Spirit's rule in his nation and over the world. Listen to, attune to and join with his yearning, as he cries:

> I long for another outpouring of the Holy Spirit, another Pentecost. That must come if things are to change in Christianity for it simply

> cannot continue in such a wretched state. The gifts and powers of the early Christian time – oh, how I long for their return! And I believe the savior is just waiting for us to ask for them.[32]

As disciples, we can assimilate every phase of the change process described in this book's earlier eight chapters. Deprived of the Holy Spirit's fullness, though, we will never live the empowered life. Samuel Chadwick issues the challenge to which we must therefore return as individuals and as a church again and again: 'That which happened at Pentecost is the biggest thing that ever happened. And now the biggest question of it all is – has it happened to you and me?'[33]

'It costs much to obtain this power [of the Holy Spirit]. It costs self-surrender and humiliation and the yielding up of our most precious things to God. It costs the perseverance of long waiting and the faith of strong trust. But when we are really in that power, we shall find this difference: that, whereas before it was hard for us to do the easiest things, now it is easy for us to do the hardest.'

A. J. Gordon[1]

'God revealed Himself to me, and I had such an experience of His love that I had to ask Him to stay His hand. I went to preaching again. The sermons were not different; I did not present any new truths, and yet hundreds were converted. I would not now be placed back where I was before that blessed experience if you should give me all the world – it would be as the small dust of the balance.'

D. L. Moody[2]

'Then Peter said, "Silver or gold I do not have, but what I have I give you. In the name of Jesus Christ of Nazareth, walk."'

Acts 3:6

10

Released

Behind our church's communion table there currently hangs a banner of Holman Hunt's Victorian painting *The Light of the World*.[3] With its exquisite artistry and colouring, the painting depicts the risen Christ who knocks at the weed-enmeshed door of our heart. The traditional evangelical invitation is for us to open our heart and invite Jesus in. In practice, scripturally, Christ as often enters our inner lives without direct invitation. To my mind, the most profoundly hopeful moment in the paschal narrative is when the risen Jesus enters a locked room full of men racked by internal conflict, guilt and crushed hopes – and administers his 'Peace' (John 20:19, 21). He has already, according to the Apostles' Creed, harrowed hell, unbidden, bringing liberation there. He will come again to an alienated individual, Thomas, who disbelieves his peers' witness, imparting revelation and release from crippling doubt. And at Pentecost the Holy Spirit will come, invading the material world with supernatural power. In all these situations, we see people caught up in what we might call 'spiritual locked-in syndrome'. Then Jesus or the Holy Spirit enters through walls of brick or flesh. The result is the same: God frees individuals and releases them into mission in the world. The movement is always from enclosure to selflessly giving oneself away.

C. S. Lewis identified this movement in his life as a becoming free from self-absorption. One result of his theistic conversion was 'a marked decrease . . . in the fussy attentiveness which I had so long paid to the progress of my own opinions and the states of my own mind'.[4] This grievous introspection can mark us both as individuals and, if the Spirit is not welcomed, as churches. We require the dynamic agency of the Spirit to bring release and call us outwards. At Pentecost the Spirit releases barred doors and shuttered windows. He brings inward joy. However, he also sends people out to impart the same liberating spirit to others. At the end of David Lean's 1946 film of *Great Expectations*, Pip returns to Miss Havisham's rotting house to find a rejected Estella preparing to embrace the same moribund life. Pip tears down the curtains, forces open the boarded windows and declares his love for Estella. Crucially, though, he leads her out of the house and into the world. At a profound level, it was this revitalizing agency that Luther and the Reformers brought to the sixteenth-century church. An authentically post-Pentecost church will always strongly move outwards. In the words of a contemporary reformer, Pope Francis, it will go to 'the existential peripheries'.[5] It will reach the edges of society, ministering especially on the margins.

At Pentecost the Holy Spirit informs this centrifugal movement in four distinct ways. First, the Spirit gives the disciples a voice. Proclamation dominates the early chapters of Acts, typified by Peter's sermon in Acts 2 in which he woos three thousand souls to Christ. Tongues of fire have fallen, releasing apostolic preaching. Disciples open their mouths and witness. The Spirit imparts boldness. The disciples have a voice because they have a subject. They preach about not the spiritual experience of being filled but the dynamic reality of Christ crucified and resurrected. The Spirit points them like an arrow to him. Peter and John declare, 'We cannot help speaking about what we have seen and heard' (Acts 4:20). From a fisherman terrified by a servant girl beside a brazier, Peter metamorphoses into an incandescent preacher and, later, a martyr who will suffer crucifixion for his Lord. His fiery preaching recalls John Wesley's words about his own preaching: 'I set myself on fire and people come and watch me burn.'[6] Peter's sermon elicits electrifying results. Thomas resisted four waves of witnesses before finally accepting the risen Christ in person; the Spirit, though, had not yet filled these witnesses. Now one Spirit-filled believer at Pentecost witnesses to the risen Christ and three thousand people receive Jesus as Lord.

Informed by his new, integrated scriptural understanding of a Messiah who came to suffer *and* for glory, Peter discharges a catalytic message. He boldly informs his Jewish audience that Jesus' death came 'by God's set purpose and foreknowledge' (Acts 2:23). What seemed like shameful, bloody defeat at the cross was Christ's triumph. Peter reinterprets Psalm 16 in messianic terms, revealing in it anticipation of a saviour whom death will not be able to hold. He links his master's passion, resurrection, ascension and Pentecost as part of one glorious divine plan. The risen Jesus furnished Peter's re-education; the coming of the Holy Spirit electrifies his understanding and propels him outwards in apostolic preaching. Thus, word and Spirit need to be central to our formation and continuing discipleship. Together, they lead us into right understanding of paschal change.

At Gethsemane the disciples abandoned the public stage for places of private refuge. Now, discovering their voice, they burst on to the public stage again. Separation from God often results in shame, fear and the need to control. After eating the apple, Adam confesses, 'I was afraid because I was naked; so I hid' (Genesis 3:10). He hides in the shadows, as we do when we seek to avoid our Father's gaze. The disciples, though, now know no shadows. Pentecost is vitalized life lived in dazzling sunlight. If ever there was a recipe for a renewed church, this is it. Such a church infused with the Spirit, holding its sail to the wind and refusing constraint, has the power to re-capture culture. We need preaching like Peter's, trumpeting Christ crucified and infused with the Spirit, as Billy Graham comments:

> I disagree . . . that we need a new jargon to appeal to this new generation. We don't at all. We need the old jargon, the biblical jargon, preached in the power and urgency of the Holy Spirit. And I believe the Holy Spirit is the communicating agent because there's something inside the human heart, when truth is preached, that says, 'Yes, that's it.'[7]

After baptismal immersion at Pentecost comes dynamic release. A. J. Gordon and D. L. Moody, in the opening quotations of this chapter, both testify to this marvellous change, including in terms of preaching. In one sense, nothing has altered. Moody proclaims the same doctrinal truths but hundreds are converted. Gordon undertakes the same tasks but with incomparable ease. Both men have passed from strenuously following Christ to surrendering to his presence and power. I believe that every human being, if they could only sense it in their soul, longs for such divine purpose and propulsion in their lives. A preacher of note before his dramatic filling on a Manhattan sidewalk, Moody still founded his ministry on human effort: 'I was all the time tugging and carrying water. But now I have a river that carries me.'[8] Now the Holy Spirit carries the disciples. They catch the current and it lifts them. The public arena, which for fifty days seemed a threat, has become a friend. The ocean in which they had threatened to drown supports them. They do not appear to make strategic choices about what to do next: 'The readiness is all.'[9] As they speak out, they are prepared for whatever the fire of the Holy Spirit and the hostility of the status quo present them with.

Such fervent proclamation always arouses opposition. The spiritual battle ensuing from apostolic preaching recalls Swiss theologian Eduard Thurneysen's words:

> To listen to a sermon is not merely a matter of being enlightened a little about God and man, but pulled into a conflict where steel clashes with steel. God's truth wishes to be victorious, and the spirit of the times and the spirit of the world must out. In every sermon that is a real sermon there is some casting out of demons.[10]

The clash of the Spirit and the demonic is observable throughout revival history. Early in Blumhardt's Black Forest ministry, he spent months of struggle before seeing God deliver a local woman from tormenting demons. Transformed, she then inspired change in another local: the irresponsible town tailor, formerly known for his sardonic tongue. Born anew, the contrite tailor led countless villagers to Blumhardt's parsonage. The expulsion of the demonic from one person had ripped the deceiving veil from the life of hidden sin of this community. This Pentecost released tongues not just in proclamation but also in responsive confession. Blumhardt's diary catalogues the escalating numbers of those visiting him to confess – 4 on

8 January 1844, 16 on 27 January, 35 on 30 January, 67 in early February, then 156 and, finally, 246 in a single day! The parents of Blumhardt's wife expressed scepticism about this spiritual awakening. Their daughter reassured them:

> There is no overstraining – nothing beyond the bounds. All is solid and real. It is the blowing of God's Spirit, a downpour of grace from on high, which quickens the inward and outward man in all his veins and gives life and soul and fills with the love of Christ.[11]

This spirit of gracious abundance marks the disciples' experience in the early chapters of Acts. Luke records that 'much grace was upon them all' (Acts 4:33). Paul identifies the paradoxical source of this grace in Jesus' essential poverty in his incarnation: 'For you know the grace of our Lord Jesus Christ, that though he was rich, yet for your sakes he became poor, so that you through his poverty might become rich' (2 Corinthians 8:9). This motif of kingdom abundance through poverty illustrates the second way that we see the Pentecostal Spirit released. Miracles are birthed in the midst of minimal human resources. The account of Peter and John healing a crippled beggar at the temple gate Beautiful reads like one of Jesus' healings. However, in his new humility, Peter says that any power manifested comes not by his effort but by the empowering presence of God. In response to the beggar's plea for money, Peter says, 'Silver or gold I do not have, but what I have I give you. In the name of Jesus Christ of Nazareth, walk' (Acts 3:6). As elsewhere (Acts 3:12, 16), Peter acknowledges his personal poverty outside the prodigious gift of the Holy Spirit. Money cannot draw this beggar from the prison of his paralysis but the name of Jesus can. We too, landed on the shore of a new calling, may have few resources for the tasks in hand. Knowing a personal Pentecost, though, we are filled with God's enabling Spirit. Peter demonstrates that, as we engage dynamically with the world, change occurs. We don't exert ourselves humanly. Our openness to emerging reality does the work for us.

We encounter this reality repeatedly in pioneering mission and revival. Arrived on new shores without financial means, we are God-dependent. Signs and wonders spring up in the wake of great faith. Stripped of our usual capacities for action, we lean on God with new abandon. Thus the nineteenth-century evangelist, Maria Woodworth-Etter, talks of a Californian revival mission that she led following her filling by the Holy Spirit:

> Here we were in a strange land and our money about gone. No means to get back east . . . We had not thought about going back till a great work had been done for the Master. We had no fear of suffering for want of means, we knew our God would supply all our needs, and his children should never be ashamed. The meeting was not advertised. The people did not know what was going to be done there. The first night twenty-three came. They felt that God was there. I told them that God had sent us there, and there would be a great work done; that hundreds would be saved. In a few days the tent would not hold the crowd that would come to hear the gospel.[12]

Poverty, expectant faith and miraculous provision converge. Woodworth-Etter did not have silver or gold, just dependency on God. As a result, her 8,000-person tent, initially thinly populated by twenty-three people, reached capacity within a matter of days. In God's upside-down kingdom, mighty things occur when human ability fails and poverty of means precipitates prayers of faith. So it was with the feeding of the five thousand from a few loaves and fish. So it was with Woodworth-Etter.

Experiencing this kingdom abundance releases the third mark of the post-Pentecost Spirit: the believers' reckless generosity with their material resources. As Kenneth Bailey, missionary to the Middle East, observes, wherever love is offered at sufficient cost, it has explosive power to change people.[13] As recipients of unmerited love, the disciples find new capacity to give themselves materially away. Luke immediately follows 'and much grace was upon them all' (Acts 4:33) with 'there were no needy persons among them' (4:34). Drawn deeper into the Godhead's family dynamics, the disciples practise radical generosity. It is not that the needs around them have changed. It is that their hearts have been sensitized to the material privation of others. This is the fruit of God's beautiful work in putting a new heart in them. In Frederick Buechner's words, their 'deep gladness and the world's deep hunger meet'.[14]

This is so important because, in a broken world, we can be tempted to take a different path. Financial historian James Buchan describes money as 'frozen desire', a commodity reflecting the (usually limited) longings of our hearts.[15] From a psychological perspective, Dorothy Rowe notes that our money decisions tend to reflect our world view and personal identity:

> Our decisions arise from a private logic hidden from others and often hidden from ourselves . . . the maintenance of ourselves as the person we know ourselves to be . . . Understanding money is a matter of understanding ourselves.[16]

At Pentecost, the Spirit seeks to free us from any imprisoning patterns of thinking that restrict us in being generous to others. These might be grounded in selfishness, greed or sheer plain fear. C. S. Lewis will echo the sentiments of many of our hearts in his confession to an American admirer whom he financially aided:

> I'm a panic-y person about money myself (which is a most shameful confession and a thing dead against Our Lord's words) and poverty frightens me more than anything else except large spiders and the tops of cliffs: one is sometimes even tempted to say that if God wanted us to live like the lilies of the field He might have given us an organism more like theirs! But of course He is right. And when you meet anyone who *does* live like the lilies, one *sees* that He is.[17]

Jesus himself defined money as possessing a personal and spiritual character. He named its binding power over us as 'Mammon' (Matthew 6:24, KJV). When money holds us captive, we root ourselves in its security instead of in God. We separate out from others, relinquishing our interdependence.

Thankfully an energizing power stronger than money exists. Money can become a blessed medium that unites. C. S. Lewis's antidote to financial anxiety was to give away all his writing royalties to people in need, often with consequences when the taxman caught up with him. The evidence of Acts is that it often takes a Spirit-filled drenching to bring many believers to this point. Entering Christ's family in a deeper way, we submit to the Spirit's baptizing and cleansing work. General Sam Houston understood this. A leader in the struggle for Texan independence, he was baptized in 1854. At his baptism in a stream, the minister suggested that Houston remove his wallet so it wouldn't get wet. Houston replied dryly that his wallet required baptism too.[18]

Andrew Murray insists that authentic Spirit filling will result in extravagant new generosity on the believer's part. Without this, something is wrong:

> So many people have given only what they could never miss and what costs them little or no sacrifice. How different it would be if the full blessing of Pentecost began to flow in. How the hearts of men would burn with love for Jesus and, out of sheer joy, be impelled to give everything so that He might be known as Saviour and so that all might know his love.[19]

The Spirit requires our agreement. In terms of financial generosity, this phase of the transformation cycle makes sacrificial demands upon us. The celebrated twentieth-century intercessor Rees Howells learned this spiritual lesson in his youth. Convicted by God of his need for full surrender, he came to realize that this included his attitude to money in his prayers for others:

> He was never again to ask God to answer a prayer through others, if He could answer it through him. That included his money. When there was a prayer for money, he must allow his own to be used. The Holy Ghost showed him that in the un-surrendered state he could spend time in asking God to supply the foreign fields and other causes, and yet not be willing for God to answer the prayer through him; and that often the Lord is 'wearied with our words'. All this unreality was to be put on one side, and the Scriptures acted on in the most practical sense.[20]

If we surrender only our hearts, and not our wallets, to God, we might reasonably be asked – to what extent are we filled with the Spirit? Have most of us received only a small measure of the Spirit in our begging bowl because we are so full of lingering fleshly desires? Rees Howells would not lie that he did not have silver or gold when he did. His financial generosity involved him frequently emptying his wallet and travelling further down a path of increasing dependency on God. So it should be with us.

How we need such counter-cultural behaviour today. What a beautiful witness to a hurting world. The Roman Emperor Julian, who despised the Christian faith, said, 'Nothing has contributed to the progress of the superstitions of the Christians as their charity to strangers . . . The impious Galileans provide not only for their own poor, but for ours as well.'[21] Historian Henry Chadwick called the practical application of Christian charity 'probably the most potent single cause of Christian success' in the ancient world.[22] A united church acting in this way spiritually flourishes and witnesses to others. Today people crave community. Yet Christian community goes further than other forms of community when costly generosity becomes its mark. Then it becomes saintly, bearing the aroma of Christ. Believers not only bond in a beautiful, sacrificial way but they exhibit winsome lives to a watching world. Let's be in no doubt: people came to believe in Jesus as Lord at Pentecost because they heard his word and experienced his outpoured presence through the Spirit. However, they also believed because, in the gratuitous generosity of the believers, they met the person of Jesus Christ himself.

We need to ask whether such a picture is purely utopian or possible today. Outside the church, its closest approximation comes in reportage from contemporary disaster zones. Rebecca Solnit, an American cultural commentator, has brilliantly described the community spirit and kindness visible in such arenas. In *A Paradise Built In Hell*, she comments that 'horrible in itself, disaster is sometimes a door back into paradise'.[23]

Such challenging borderlands can impel us to become 'our sister's and brother's keeper' afresh:[24]

> These remarkable societies suggest that, just as many machines reset themselves to their original settings after a power outage, so human beings reset themselves to something altruistic, communitarian, resourceful, and imaginative after a disaster, that we revert to something we already know how to do. The possibility of paradise is already within us as a default setting.[25]

Although Solnit is a secular writer, she quotes a telling account of 9/11 by Father James Martin, a Jesuit priest. Consider his description of his experience at Ground Zero, observing how it mirrors the communitarian unity of the believers at Pentecost:

> I have to say, for me, working down there has been the most profound experience of the Holy Spirit that I've ever had. It's a feeling, of course, but it's also a very strong feeling and it's an experience that I've not really had before. Essentially, for me, even from the first day, I felt this enormous sense of unity and friendship and concord and amity, and everyone working together . . . On top of that, everybody was kind and patient and generous and helpful. I didn't hear one argument the whole time I was down there. It was really striking. You just got the sense – for me as a Christian – of the Kingdom of God. This is the Kingdom, this is the notion of everyone working and living together and eating together and pulling for a cause – totally other-directed, totally selfless and, frankly, very self-deprecating.[26]

What a beautiful picture amid tragedy. What a picture of the Spirit ministering amid ruins. Solnit's thesis is that natural disasters remove inhibiting social structures and behaviours, freeing people to rediscover the communitarian instinct that is our natural default setting. By contrast, it is the Holy Spirit, not disaster, who precipitates such behaviour at Pentecost. We know that such behaviour after a disaster typically reverts to its previous state over time. The Acts believers, though, do not falter in their commitment to each other and their ceaseless activity for the kingdom.

In all this, they are bound together in loving unity, the fourth mark of the post-Pentecost Spirit. They return to society from Toynbee's state of 'withdrawal' and pursue the family intimacy of God. Thus, in the Believers' Prayer in Acts 4:24–31, they pray to God, the 'Sovereign Lord' who 'made the heaven and the earth and the sea, and everything in them'; they ask for power to heal 'through the name of your holy servant Jesus'; and they are again 'all filled with the Holy Spirit' and speak God's word boldly. Whereas each disciple heard Jesus' initial call as a personal invitation, they now understand that they are part of a larger pattern. This movement into deeper relational life has increased exponentially in the phases of this book's last four chapters. Acts 4:32 states, 'All the believers were one in heart and mind', that is, in tune and, in the Greek etymology, spiritually breathing together. Their beautiful interdependence is one of the gifts that they bear as they now re-enter society.

Jon Tyson, who has planted a series of parish churches throughout Manhattan, describes the potential of such community in our culture: 'A creative minority is a Christian community in a web of stubbornly loyal relationships, knotted together in a living network of persons, who are committed to practicing the way of Jesus for the renewal of the world.'[27] The post-Pentecost borderland invites us to grow relationally far beyond what we have imagined for ourselves. We see this in our age in liminal twelve-step groups and, in a more profound way, Christian communities like the Bruderhof and L'Arche. How revival community begins is always intriguing. The Acts community forms through a kind of bottom-up, dispersed leadership. No single person commands the disciples. The Holy Spirit orchestrates them in a perfect synergy of personalities and gifts. This constitutes a marked difference from their in-fighting and competition during Jesus' earthly ministry. Dispersed, shared leadership often seems to prevail in times of revival. Through it, God catalyses 'the priesthood of all believers', in contrast to what may be possible via top-down leadership of the traditional kind.

Thus in 1900, Evan Roberts, future enabler of the Welsh Revival, began forming prayer gatherings to train young men to participate in public worship. His conviction was that 'no one is to lead the meeting, but each one is to take part as moved by the Spirit'.[28] Such practice marked the meetings that he led throughout the Welsh Revival. The emphasis of this awakening was on cultivating and experiencing God's presence. Meetings were spontaneous, characterized by the Spirit's leading and dominated more by prayer, worship and testimonies than by lengthy preaching:

> The meetings open – after any amount of singing while the congregation is assembling – by the reading of a chapter or a psalm. Then it is go-as-you-please for two hours or more. And the amazing thing is that it does go, and does not entangle in what seems to be inevitable confusion. Three-fourths of the meeting consists of singing. No one uses a hymn book. No one gives out a hymn. The last person to control the meetings in any way is Mr. Evan Roberts. People pray and sing, give testimony, exhort as the Spirit moves them. As a study of the psychology of crowds, I have seen nothing like it. You feel that the thousand

> or fifteen hundred persons before you have become merged into one myriad-headed but single-souled personality.[29]

Our cultural understanding of calling is often individualistic. Pentecostal calling, by contrast, involves a group of people lifting their eyes simultaneously to God. This is what revival preacher Duncan Campbell characterized as the mark of revival: 'a community saturated with God'.[30] This Pentecost community will be the generative force that births the early church.

When the Holy Spirit rests on a community, people cannot leave church meetings; they pray long into the night and linger in one another's homes – not from piety but reluctance to be apart from others. Calling becomes an issue of character as much as action, as people relationally rediscover themselves. In this liminal phase, everything is in motion, and yet there seems to be no chaos, only cohesion. A deeper order is at play, one possible when conventional structures and practices dissolve. Often captive to fear since Gethsemane, we now surrender to the Holy Spirit's power. He carries us, removing inhibiting walls between normally separate groups. He assures spontaneous prayer support from others when opposition threatens any individual.

The writer of Hebrews prays, 'May the God of peace . . . equip you with everything good for doing his will' (13:20–21). At Pentecost, God's equipping Spirit resources us in these four ways described. The Greek word for 'equip' (*katartisai*) recalls the setting right of a broken bone or the putting of a dislocated bone back into place. The Spirit's equipping, therefore, represents not some deformation of our being but a return to what Rebecca Solnit described as our 'original setting', made as we are in the image of God. We reset to the default setting within us. Our communitarian unity leads to countless small acts of kindness, as we see in the pages of Acts. The anthropologist Margaret Mead, who spent her career researching prehistoric peoples, used to ask audiences, 'What is the earliest sign of civilization?'[31] In response to their answers ('a clay pot', 'iron tools'), she claimed that it was a healed leg bone. Such healings were never found in the remains of early, warring societies, she said: 'But the healed femur showed that someone must have cared for the injured person – hunted on his behalf, brought him food, and served him at personal sacrifice.' While Roman society discarded unwanted babies on its rubbish dumps, the Holy Spirit breathed loving kindness into believers.

My colleague Simon Ponsonby believes that contemporary psychologists should add to their diagnostic charts the category 'loss of glory'. It is glory that humankind lost at the fall, knowing only alienation thereafter. It is glory that is restored at Pentecost when the Holy Spirit comes. But it is quiet, humble, servant-hearted glory, not the glory of the triumphal arch or the conquering hero. The acts of kindness at Pentecost are not the results of a welfare state, institutionalized charity or Big Society, but the fruit of the Spirit, outflowing in love. Of course, any paradise regained will incur new opposition, both political and spiritual in source. Persecution will mushroom. At a political level, the dissolving of conventional hierarchies will incense a ruling status quo. None of that, though, can obscure the beauty of the Spirit's work, or forestall the final return and fulfilled reign of Christ. At Pentecost, simple kindness, generosity and love turn a mean-hearted, crucifying world upside down. How our church needs fully to inhabit this borderland again. When we do, we will prize Pentecost not for our personal joy but for the ongoing redemption of our world. Our faces will be set outwards in joy and we will reach 'the existential peripheries', one and all.

'Am I ignitable? God deliver me from the dread asbestos of "other things". Saturate me with the oil of the Spirit that I may be a flame.'

Jim Elliot[1]

'Depend upon it – you will find in your own life you may have many days of heaven upon earth, but the place of persecution and rejection will be the spot where Jesus Christ manifests Himself most to you.'

Charles Spurgeon[2]

'Stephen was an ordinary man made extraordinary in God. You may be very ordinary, but God wants to make you extraordinary in the Holy Ghost. God is ready to touch and to transform you right now.'

Smith Wigglesworth[3]

11

Igniting

This chapter details the final phase of the transformation cycle. It is a phase in which, if we have known Pentecost's full blessing, our eyes will turn outwards in mission. As the angels said at Jesus' ascension, direct your eyes away from a simple longing for heaven. Turn them to this world's needs and seek the Holy Spirit's power to realize heaven on earth. The post-ascension community's behaviour in this phase, whether in Stephen's impassioned advocacy for Christ or the believers' fidelity after their aggressive dispersal from Jerusalem, demonstrates the paschal-shaped life to which we are called. Some of the believers will see significant ministry fruit in their lifetimes. Others' harvest will come later. All, however, are possessed by a passionate purpose and the grip of God's distinctive call on their lives. In this phase, we know the unmistakable conviction that our lives bear meaning and will yield fruit. Living into this discipleship stage, we can be assured of God's 'Well done, good and faithful servant!' (Matthew 25:23).

In the book of Acts, we see men and women seized by compelling faith. The potential challenges of this discipleship stage are twofold. The first is compromise personally or from within the body of believers; the second is hostile opposition from without. Our task is to safeguard and share this new life, resisting internal erosion or external persecution. Each possibility brings with it contestation and painful consequences, and the image of the Holy Spirit as fire underlines the elemental nature involved in each.

In relation to compromise, the Pentecostal image of fire suggests both volatility and integrity of nature, one purifying and expulsive. The Spirit's fire at Pentecost demands resilience and diamond-like probity in the believers. It must hold to its essential nature. It will not tolerate counterfeits. That is why, in the opening chapters of Acts, we encounter two examples of contaminating influence that the Spirit will not brook. Jim Elliot, the young missionary martyred by the Auca Indians in 1956, understood the Spirit's fire. While still a student at Wheaton College, he wrote in his diary: '"He makes His ministers a flame of fire." Am I ignitable? God deliver me from the dread asbestos of "other things". Saturate me with the oil of the Spirit that I may be a flame.'[4] As disciples we can know either the flame of God's fire or the flame-resistant effects of 'spiritual asbestos'. Elliot devoted himself to cultivating an 'ignitable' life, rooting out compromise within. Electing to live a life of purity, he continues to ignite the hearts of many called to the mission field in remote places.

Fire, though, can also threaten an asbestos-minded status quo. Ignited calling carries us to a new edge, one often threatening to the established order. Only the second chapter of Arthur Wallis's classic book on revival, *In the Day of Thy Power*, emphasizes that revival is always 'a sign spoken against'.[5] If some people at Pentecost merely mock the disciples for being drunk, we subsequently read of the authorities' progressive opposition. Gloriously, not a single disciple falls away or retreats under attack. Filled with God's fire, when challenged, their fire divides and travels elsewhere. These are men and women in their spiritual element, unquenchable. Even when they pay a price by persecution or death, their influence only knows creative increase. God paradoxically builds his early church through the engine of persecution. In the title of F. F. Bruce's Acts commentary, a movement that could have been stamped into the ashes becomes instead 'the spreading flame'.[6]

The image of fire, fluid and mercurial, also speaks of the flexibility required of us in this discipleship stage. Peter's world turns upside down in a day when he visits Cornelius' house and discovers that God intends the gospel for the Gentiles. Peter does not insist on his existing paradigm. He observes God moving in this new situation and allows his world view to be reshaped. His receptivity is grounded in sensitivity to the Spirit's flow both within and without him. Peter's inner and outer worlds enjoy perfect symmetry. Our spiritual vision broadens and deepens in this phase. The Spirit removes walls circumscribing our perception. This phase of personal change is thus wonderfully creative. Whereas we formerly lived by deadening habit, now we move in step with the Spirit. We resist strategizing our way into new life but remain open to unfolding, emergent reality. We know the truth of Jesus' words in Revelation 21:5: 'I am making everything new!' We innovate rather than copy, sensitive to the urgent needs around us. We are in dynamic conversation with a world that we are discovering afresh.

Why would any believer resist such an attractive path and court internal compromise? David Whyte hints at the kind of temptation that may have assailed Ananias and Sapphira, in their example of classic compromise in the opening chapters of Acts:

> There is a certain kind of heaviness and insulation we can grow used to. The body can feel strange when it inhabits the world in a lighter way, when it encounters a form of happiness or fulfillment for which it has had no apprenticeship. A lightness and litheness that gives us a sense of ease, movement and potential may bring things that have always been a struggle to us more easily, and scare us to death in the process.[7]

Ananias and Sapphira cannot relinquish this heaviness. They fear embracing an 'unbearable lightness of being'. They will not accept dispossession and simplification. Their fate has been described as brutal in the past and continues to read as such to some in our age. However, it testifies, like it or not, to the importance of personal integrity and corporate solidarity in this stage of spiritual growth. There simply isn't room for believers to speak half-truths or deceive each other. In this phase, God's holiness will not brook any compromise. The issue perhaps less concerns money per se than Ananias' and Sapphira's refusal to surrender themselves fully to Christ. They are not abandoned. The fact that they are already enfolded believers and not simply spectating seekers makes the issue doubly corrosive.

Simon the Magician, another compromising agent amid the apostolic community, recalls many charlatans of our own New Age. Adoring crowds exclaim, 'This man is the divine power known as the Great Power' (Acts 8:10). His offer of money for the gift of the Holy Spirit demonstrates several persistently destructive elements witnessed in historical revivals: human appropriation of the power of the Spirit as something to be bought and managed; a pursuit of power for power's sake; relationally unaccountable ministry that seeks its own ends; and an attempt personally to incarnate spiritual power, becoming 'the Great Power', instead of acknowledging one's creaturely separateness from God.

As Thomas Aquinas said, 'Whatever is received . . . is received according to the mode of the receiver.'[8] At Pentecost God blesses us with a most precious gift. The disciples, tempered by their paschal trials, receive it with humility and gratitude. By contrast, Ananias, Sapphira and Simon demean the gift. Their moral and spiritual filter system is contaminated. So we too, in this phase, must ask tough questions of ourselves about any latent resistance to the Holy Spirit's purifying work. We need to interrogate our motives. Why do we seek the Spirit's empowering? From a longing to identify with Christ's self-giving on the cross or for our own appropriation? When we seek to bless others through exercising the Spirit's gifts, is this for our glory or for God's glory?

Repeatedly, Christian history demonstrates the close link between personal integrity and the Spirit's uncompromising reign. As the pastor of a Lancashire chapel, the young Samuel Chadwick discovered that he was unconsciously pursuing 'a false aim in my work. I lived and laboured for my sermons, and was unfortunately more concerned about their excellence and reputation than the repentance of the people.'[9] Recognizing his pride and reliance on human methods, he set fire to his treasured sermons one night and was immediately released in the Holy Spirit:

> I could not explain what had happened, but it was a bigger thing than I had ever known. There came into my soul a deep peace, a thrilling joy, and a new sense of power. My mind was quickened. I felt I had received a new faculty of understanding. Every power was vitalized. My body was quickened. There was a new sense of

> spring and vitality, a new power of endurance and a strong man's exhilaration in big things.[10]

Chadwick's next sermon resulted in seven conversions. The following Sunday, many in his church experienced a baptism in the Holy Spirit. Within months, revival had spread, with hundreds converted. Chadwick had set up camp in a place of integrity. The Holy Spirit seeks a clean vessel. The disciples in Acts remain pure conductors of the heat of the Spirit. Those seeking to appropriate the heat for their own ends get burned up.

We now turn to the clash between the Spirit-filled believers and the status quo. William Barclay defined New Testament Christians as a people 'completely fearless, absurdly happy, and in constant trouble'.[11] Jesus persistently emphasizes the likelihood of our enduring opposition. His first seven beatitudes seek to conform us as a community of love. In the eighth ('Blessed are those who are persecuted because of righteousness, for theirs is the kingdom of heaven', Matthew 5:10), he turns outwards to contemplate the non-Christian world's response to us. He reveals that self-giving community comes at a cost. The world stoned Jesus and, as we seek to identify with his beauty, may well stone us. In John 21:18, Jesus paints for Peter two compelling portraits of different seasons of Christian discipleship. In the first, he portrays the young man who dresses himself and goes where he wants. This describes our youthful discipleship, a time of autonomy and self-will. In the second, he portrays the older man who has others dress him (for the cross) and lead him where he does not want to go. This is mature discipleship that knows renunciation. St John ends his Gospel with Jesus preparing Peter for martyrdom. Having done this, Jesus says to Peter for a final time, 'Follow me!' (John 21:19). What we understand by this command compared with the same words spoken to Philip at the start of Jesus' ministry (John 1:43) speaks eloquently of how far Peter and we have travelled along the paschal road.

In this phase of mature discipleship, Jesus speaks of a spirituality of living opposed. At the same time, he never says that opposition is our goal. We need to reject a distorted theology that would court suffering and persecution. Rather, in this stage Jesus invites us further into his love, a place from which we can operate with new strength even in the face of opposition. Knowing the depths of his love for us, we meet the world's evil by imitating his grace. We are never to understand dying to self or as a martyr purely for their grievous cost. Instead, each signals the extent to which we have surrendered to God's love and refuse to turn away from witnessing that love to others.

Although it is not every believer's calling to suffer martyrdom, increasingly Christians in the West face opposition. The world can demand that we turn the wine of our faith into water and refuse to live in the fullness of who God has called us to be. Scripture offers us different pictures of how to interact with the culture. Daniel and his friends embrace a Nazirite lifestyle, modelling lives of integrity while engaging shrewdly with systems of power. Stephen in Acts 6 – 7 raises his prophetic voice to the authorities, refusing to be muzzled. His example has often inspired the young. Rembrandt's first signed painting (1625), created at the age of nineteen, depicts Stephen meeting his death.[12] Women and men in the mission field have likewise drawn strength from Stephen's example.

I write from a city crammed with churches (thirty Anglican ones and many of other vibrant denominations). Oxford's history records both dynamic Christian activity *and* crushing persecution. St Frideswide, a holy female warrior for Christ, founded the first Christian community here amid brutal threat and opposition. Latimer, Ridley and Cranmer died at the stake. John Wesley, founder of the Methodists and a Christ Church tutor, was confronted at his college gates in 1733 by an angry mob. The last fifteen years in Oxford have seen flourishing church activity and the vocal presence of the New Atheism. Meanwhile, extreme global persecution increases, especially in Africa and Asia. In a Sunday evening service in summer 2016, Charlie Cleverly, rector of St Aldates, asked a visiting Nigerian bishop who had been studying for a year in Oxford for his departing message to our church. The bishop replied, 'Do not compromise the faith in the West that we are dying for in Africa.' As he spoke these words, the Holy Spirit fell. Our Pastor of Theology, Simon Ponsonby, sensing this as God's word for us, never preached the sermon that he had prepared. We suspended the normal order of service and experienced a prolonged period of Spirit-led worship and ministry instead.

The bishop was underlining that there aren't two churches, one free and one persecuted. We are one church. Moreover, persecution constitutes an attack upon Jesus Christ himself. As Jesus says to Saul, as the latter presses towards Damascus to attack and imprison Jesus' followers, 'Saul, Saul, why do you persecute me?' (Acts 9:4). The second letter of Timothy reveals that true godliness and persecution are inseparable: 'Everyone who wants to live a godly life in Christ Jesus will be persecuted' (3:12). How then do we steward this new life that we enjoy? How do we maintain our voice in the West? What can we learn from Stephen's example?

Stephen possesses a voice of spiritual authority, first, because he is anchored in God's word. He knows the story in which he is living. This is vital in a postmodern age that discredits any metanarrative. The Bible describes a world history that is meaningful and coherent in the context of God's unfolding purposes. Stephen's opponents, men steeped in the Mosaic law, accuse him of undermining the law and the temple. In response, Stephen recounts the history of Israel through key forebears, challenging the Sanhedrin's world view. He effortlessly draws on the books of Genesis, Exodus, Deuteronomy, Isaiah and Amos. More than just rebut their charges against him, Stephen speaks with prophetic power. He critiques the Sanhedrin's reading of Scripture, arguing that they have rejected the Messiah Jesus who comes to supersede the temple. Words spoken by the Polish Catholic poet Czeslaw Milosz, who knew well what it was to live under oppression during the Nazi occupation of Poland, capture the impact of Stephen's words on his accusers: 'In a room where people unanimously maintain a conspiracy of silence, one word of truth sounds like a pistol shot.'[13] Indeed, Stephen's example recalls the lives of many Eastern bloc dissidents who similarly valiantly challenged oppressive status quos.

Those who know the truth of which they speak cannot remain silent. In a culture of liquid bonds and political lies, truth becomes immensely powerful, not just a compass for personal survival but a vehicle for societal transformation. This is the reason that Peter's sermon can convert three thousand at Pentecost when not a single conversion had been recorded in Scripture during the preceding fifty days. God speaks through his word, and his word is the word of truth.

Second, Stephen has a voice of authority because his eyes are trained on Jesus, the Word made flesh. Stephen's voice is anchored not just in a story but a person. We are relational people and the ultimate relationship that we can know and within which we flourish is with Jesus. Stephen cleaves close to Christ. His radical pursuit of his master recalls many elements of Jesus' own life. Scripture first reports Stephen as a man who humbly waits on tables (Acts 6:2–6), recalling

Jesus' washing of his disciples' feet. Like Jesus in his oppressors' hands, Stephen speaks truth, forgives his enemies and lets go of his life. Spurgeon views Stephen's death as full of Jesus: 'Jesus seen', 'Jesus invoked', 'Jesus trusted' and 'Jesus imitated'.[14] This heartfelt trust and obedience represents a vital new type of consciousness permeating the post-Pentecost world.

Stephen arrives at a crossroads in his life. He decides that nothing will make him conspire in the diminishment of his faith and self. Both of these threaten to occur if he remains silent. Instead, he speaks out, including forgivingly for his persecutors. His life culminates with an astonishing vision of an open heaven: the glory of God visible and Jesus standing by his Father's side. Jesus had earlier told the Sanhedrin at his own trial, 'You will see the Son of Man sitting at the right hand of the Mighty One' (Mark 14:62). Now Stephen offers the first New Testament testimony of the reality of the ascended Jesus. Stephen affirms that Jesus is exactly where he predicted he would be, at God's right hand. In short, Jesus is exactly the Saviour that he claimed to be. Jesus himself responds by standing to Stephen, of which Smith Wigglesworth says:

> Jesus was so keenly interested in that martyr, Stephen, that he stood up. May the Lord open our eyes to see him and to know that he is deeply interested in all that concerns us. He is touched with the feeling of our infirmities.[15]

This is surely Jesus' response to every martyr who dies by the flame, sword, noose or bullet, or whatever other foul means of execution a hostile world employs. Jesus honours his beloved bride, and these men and women, by their faith and fortitude in death, testify to God's grace to a broken world.

We can ask for nothing deeper to sustain us in the face of opposition than a vision from heaven. Stephen already belongs to another world and thus walks unconstrained by pressure from this one. We need eternity's perspective. Otherwise we will interpret things narrowly and lack larger courage. Classical paintings depicting Stephen's death fall into two categories: those depicting only his stoning and those incorporating his vision of Jesus standing in heaven. The former merely record a brutal reality that we see nightly in the shattered bodies of our TV news broadcasts. The latter offer transcendent context. Our faith is not a matter of political decision or worldly commitment. It is anchored in our understanding of matters eternal and in knowing that our ultimate destiny resides in heaven.

Third, Stephen's voice cannot be silenced because the Holy Spirit gives him words of fire. We need voices anchored in Scripture and an intimate knowledge of Jesus. However, it is the Holy Spirit who imparts words of courage, conviction and penetrating truth in the face of the powers that be. Jesus tells his disciples:

> On my account you will be brought before governors and kings as witnesses to them and to the Gentiles. But when they arrest you, do not worry about what to say or how to say it. At that time you will be given what to say, for it will not be you speaking, but the Spirit of your Father speaking through you.
> (Matthew 10:18–20)

Luke reports Stephen as one of several men chosen as deacons 'who are known to be full of the Spirit and wisdom' (Acts 6:3), 'a man full of faith and of the Holy Spirit' (6:5), 'a man full of God's grace and power' (6:8) and a man whom the Synagogue of Freedmen cannot defeat in verbal battle, given 'his wisdom or the Spirit by whom he spoke' (6:10). It is hard to think of any biblical figure about whom there are such rich associations of the Spirit, except Jesus himself. How I'd love to have met this inspired man, one marinated in the Holy Spirit. Full of the Spirit, he is indeed 'given what to say' in his time of trial. He speaks without notes and with magisterial authority, as if the Spirit rests on him like a tongue of fire and ignites his speech.

This is truth against which there is no defence. Stephen's listeners cannot withstand what they hear and retreat into denial. Unable to marshal their own words, they resort to their only weapon: violence. This represents one face of persecution: overt attack. Acts 8:3 reports of Saul's ensuing persecution of the Jerusalem believers: 'Saul began to destroy the church.' The Greek verb 'destroy' recalls the ruin and devastation caused by an army, even in Psalm 80:13 by a wild boar ravaging a vineyard. However, we need to be alert to subtler registers in which worldwide persecution can operate. In the West, the Persecutor does not have mobs beat us up or burn down our churches. As Nik Ripken notes, the Persecutor's tactics are often quieter.[16] He shapes a toxic culture in which family, friends or bosses can pressure us into remaining silent, our faith becoming 'personal' and 'private'. Pope Francis terms this 'polite persecution', one aspect of the changing context of Christianity in a determinedly secular culture.[17]

Stephen therefore models three aspects of finding our voice as mature disciples: through being grounded in Scripture, hidden in Christ and empowered by the Spirit. He offers a brilliantly illuminated foil to the shadowy disciples who fled Gethsemane. He accepts a bitter cup given to him to drink, just as his master did. He knows the truth of Jesus' words, 'Everyone will hate you because of me' (Mark 13:13, NIV 2011). However, he also discovers the comforting truth of Jesus' promise that 'the Holy Spirit will teach you at that time what you should say' (Luke 12:12). Cleaving to Christ, Stephen refuses to divorce his deep gladness and the world's deep hunger. Instead he speaks out, despite threat of violence. Like Bonhoeffer, returning to Germany on a course that will lead directly to the hangman's noose, Stephen discovers that suffering is 'the badge of true discipleship'.[18] He embraces the prophetic calling on his life and, through his death, marvellously glorifies God.

In persecuting countries on the World Watch List today, Christians face similar martyrdom. Like Jesus, for the joy set before them, they endure the cross. It will take time for the full extent of stories to emerge from the blood-stained territories overrun by ISIS. However, we can see them anticipated in the testimony of Jonathan Goforth, a Canadian Presbyterian missionary, who witnessed revival and persecution in early twentieth-century China. In *By My Spirit*, Goforth writes of meeting an eminent Chinese scholar who tells him, with tears in his eyes, 'I am convinced that there can be no salvation for us sinners except through the Redeemer, Jesus Christ.'[19]

The scholar reveals that he was led to look into the Bible and came to a saving faith after witnessing a massacre in the governor's residence at Taiyuanfu in 1900. He happened to be in the governor's courtyard when soldiers herded in some sixty missionaries to await execution. He was struck by their utter fearlessness in this situation. There was no panic or cries for mercy. They waited on death with perfect calm. Then a golden-haired girl of thirteen stepped forward to address the governor:

> 'Why are you planning to kill us?' she asked, her voice carrying to the farthest corner of the courtyard. 'Haven't our doctors come from far off lands to give their lives for your people? Many with hopeless diseases have been healed; some who were blind have

> received their sight, and health and happiness have been brought into thousands of your homes because of what our doctors have done. Is it because of this good that has been done that you are going to kill us?' The governor's head was down. He had nothing to say. There was really nothing he could say. She continued: 'Governor, you talk a lot about filial piety. It is your claim, is it not, that among the hundred virtues filial piety takes the highest place. But you have hundreds of young men in this province who are opium sots and gamblers. Can they exercise filial piety? Can they love their parents and obey their will? Our missionaries have come from foreign lands and have preached Jesus to them, and He has saved them and given them power to live rightly and to love and obey their parents. Is it then, perhaps, because of this good that has been done that we are to be killed?'[20]

The Chinese scholar reports how the governor writhed under this attack, like the Sanhedrin before Stephen. However, this dramatic standoff lasted only a moment:

> A soldier, standing near the girl, grasped her by the hair, and with one blow of his sword severed her head from her body. That was the signal for the massacre to begin. 'I saw fifty-nine men, women, and children killed that afternoon,' said the scholar. 'Even in the very moment of death every face seemed to hold a smile of peace. I saw one lady speaking cheerfully to a little boy who was clinging to her hand. Then her turn came, and her body fell to the yamen floor. But the little fellow, without the sign of a whimper on his face, stood straight upright, still holding fast his mother's hand. Then another blow, and the little mangled corpse lay beside that of the mother. Is it any wonder, therefore, that such marvellous fortitude should have led me to search your Scriptures and to have compelled me to believe that the Bible is in very truth the Word of God?'[21]

This girl's luminous innocence reminds one of Stephen's almost child-like directness. Such innocence comes from a deep abiding in Christ. It speaks of secure attachment, a resting on Jesus' breast and ensuing words of prophetic truth. Humbling and beyond the apparent capacity of many of us, such behaviour is deep discipleship's fruit. How beautiful. How devastating. How wholly like Christ. Perhaps caught between faith and compromise in our lives, we can only marvel. However, this is the life available to any Christian empowered in a time of contestation by the Holy Spirit.

'Life shrinks or expands in proportion to one's courage,' writes Anais Nin.[22] It only remains to be asked if such courage represents a foolhardy act, a waste of life. Scripture insists not, celebrating any death lived righteously that glorifies God. To answer this, however, is to approach one of Scripture's profoundest paradoxes: that persecution frequently catalyses the gospel's spread. The persecution that follows Stephen's martyrdom results in a great scattering of believers from Jerusalem into the world. This precisely achieves what Jesus commanded in Acts 1:8 – the taking of the gospel to 'all Judea and Samaria, and to the ends of the earth'. Prominent in this persecution, of course, is Saul who guards the clothes of those stoning Stephen and 'giving approval to his death' (Acts 8:1). Saul, who hears Stephen petition Jesus about his killers, 'Lord, do not hold this sin against them' (Acts 7:60), then meets Jesus on the Damascus road. How extraordinary to observe that Saul now experiences Jesus' forgiveness there. At Stephen's behest, Jesus forgives a man complicit in Stephen's death. Augustine himself conjectured that Saul's conversion was due to this prayer of Stephen being heard.[23] Stephen's dying words enable Saul's new birth. In short, we owe the early church, huge sections of the New Testament and one of its greatest saints to Stephen's cleaving to Christ. A single human life has an impact on the entire unfolding of church history.

Stephen's life demonstrates that no-one can control where the Spirit of self-giving love will lead a person. His life also reveals that you cannot control what the world's reaction to you will ever be. It is too easy to adopt a triumphalist theology of Pentecost. The book of Acts suggests that the Spirit comes to empower us as much for persecution as for proclamation. Jesus on the cross and Stephen at his stoning demonstrate how to live in the face of worldly wrath. Peter's future death as a martyr will 'glorify God' (John 21:19). Stephen looks up just before his stoning to witness 'the glory of God' (Acts 7:55). At the threshold of death, these men do not experience defeat but are gathered up in God's glory. In the battle between fire and asbestos, they embrace fire's elemental power. They are ignitable, they burn brightly and they ignite others. Theirs is a love that continues to give us hope today.

'When we have occasion to lament the spiritual poverty immediately around us, we may be sure that the bird that has forsaken us is singing his lovely song, to somebody else's rapture, on a distant bough. And so it shall continue until that day dawns for which the Church has ever prayed, when the Holy Dove shall feel equally at home on every shore and the earth shall be filled with the knowledge of the glory of the Lord as the waters cover the sea.'

F. W. Boreham[1]

'Lo, he comes with clouds descending,
Once for our salvation slain;
Thousand thousand saints attending
Swell the triumph of his train:
Alleluia! Alleluia! Alleluia!
Christ the Lord returns to reign.'

Charles Wesley[2]

'Let God have your life;
He can do more with it than you can.'

D. L. Moody[3]

12
Conclusion

Does life possess inherent meaning? Is it informed by transcendent purpose? The atheist will answer, 'No'; our attempts to discover meaningful narrative to our lives are delusional fictions. Much of the memorable quality of Jacob Epstein's *Lazarus* comes from its multi-contextual power; the interpretations that it offers derive as much from its specific position in the foyer of New College chapel, Oxford, as from the sculpture itself. Thus, it stands with its raised body facing the secular world beyond the west door, head rolled backwards towards the east chapel with its worship of God. The sculpture seems to depict contemporary humanity, gazing back at a disappearing world of faith, perhaps wistfully, perhaps in disbelief or contempt. The worshipful world of the chapel reads as a death from which we need to escape. Julian Barnes, an atheist sometimes nostalgic for God, comments that 'doctors, priests and novelists conspire to present human life as a story progressing to a meaningful conclusion'. By contrast, he ripostes:

> If, as we approach death and look back on our lives, we 'understand our narrative' and stamp a final meaning upon it, I suspect we are doing little more than confabulating: processing strange, incomprehensible, contradictory input into some kind, any kind, of believable story – but believable mainly to ourselves. I do not object to this atavistic need for narrative – not least since it is how I make my living – but I am suspicious of it.[4]

The work of Marie de Hennezel, caring intimately for people at the end of their lives, refutes this claim. De Hennezel believes that our lives contain an inbuilt narrative discoverable before death. She sees a dying patient's telling of their story as fundamental to their living out well their final days on earth:

> There is a need to give shape to one's life and to show this shape, which gives it its meaning, to someone else. Once the telling of it has been accomplished, the person seems to be able to let go, and die.[5]

For the atheist, the great fifty-day cycle symbolizes a flawed attempt to ascribe divine meaning to human existence. Christians, though, see it as the very signature of God in creation, the deep structure beneath all other structures, the process by which new life rises from death's ashes, and the entry point into human flourishing. Amid the rich interpretations that it yields, Epstein's *Lazarus* offers its richest truth when viewed from a seat within New College chapel. The figure stands, our forerunner outside the chapel, poised in front of the west door, about to go out to love and serve the Lord in the world, head turned back to us in invitation. We too need to hear the commanding word of God, die to ourselves, walk out of our tombs and bring fresh life to a twilight, secular world.

The paschal narrative encompasses God's deepest truths about personal and corporate transformation. It surpasses anything that I know from psychology, anthropology, literature or other faiths. Its change process involves us in periods of disorientation and bewilderment as well as breathless joy and dynamic release. It leads us through multiple borderlands and has been described as a 'pilgrim's progress', a journey down 'ancient paths' and a 'crossing the unknown sea'. Adventure, uncertainty and thrilling arrival coalesce in this journey.

What spiritual lessons does Scripture offer for navigating this cycle? One is that, possessing the paschal map, we learn to live into the continuing processes of death and renewal. We grow spiritually as we increase in resilience negotiating these cycles:

> The double entendre of threshold is fitting. A threshold is a place of passage, a portal through which we pass from here to here and from known to unknown. But it also means a measure of endurance. If we can increase our threshold for crossing thresholds, then we can transcend some of the limits of life, and we can change our lives in the most prodigious ways.[6]

Rather than avoiding these liminal borderlands, we court them as places of spiritual renewal. We embrace, rather than seek to 'manage', the change cycle. We discover that this is an ongoing pilgrim journey of discipleship to which Jesus calls us. The 'great cloud of witnesses' in Hebrews 12:1 are saints who have learned to dwell in such places, there extracting their deepest insights about God's faithfulness and love.

The second lesson from Scripture is that this journey, although existentially lonely at times, is to be travelled with others. Jesus' final words at Lazarus' raising are to the community: 'Loose him and let him go' (John 11:44, KJV). The paschal journey is not some solipsistic path of self-individuation but an invitation into a community of restoration and love. We need to know and live into this story, and we need to travel it together, drawing on the support of others and offering our encouragement to others in turn.

This final chapter, though, will probe Scripture's third most essential lesson of the great fifty days. For if the disciples do not always travel this journey well, Jesus, by contrasts, models it perfectly. In his living, dying and rising, Jesus is therefore our beautiful example. As Henri Nouwen observes: 'There is no journey to God outside of the journey that Jesus made.'[7] Jesus furnishes us with a master character lesson in humility, the virtue enabling us to meet change in the most fulfilled way possible:

> Do nothing out of selfish ambition or vain conceit, but in humility consider others better than yourselves. Each of you should look not only to your own interests, but also to the interests of others. Your attitude should be the same as that of Christ Jesus:
>
> Who, being in very nature God
> did not consider equality with God something
> to be grasped,
> but made himself nothing,
> taking the very nature of a servant,
> being made in human likeness.
> And being found in appearance as a man,
> he humbled himself
> and became obedient to death – even death on a cross!
>
> (Philippians 2:3–8)

Humility is intrinsic to God's nature. Charismatics often emphasize God's power, but we might better stress his humility.

The main reason that we are to court humility is not because we are creatures (that is, not God), although that forms an important secondary reason, but because humility is the Godhead's essence. God's very nature is to be humble, descending and self-giving. Jesus' transformation came through surrender to descent. Cultivating humility shapes us for the paschal journey.

Humility runs counter to both inflation and deflation in human character. It is about neither grandiosity nor false piety, a putting down of oneself. It demands a robust ego that can be tempered in the service of others' good. Jesus' humble nature gave him an infectiously natural ease in his downward journey from heaven to death on a cross. Humility presumes grounded realism, a seeing of things as they really are. It is fully consistent with an ability to be assertive, authoritative or to express righteous anger. Jesus was the humblest man who ever lived ('for I am gentle and humble in heart', Matthew 11:29), yet he overthrew tables and expelled temple money-lenders. Above all, it is a character trait to be embodied rather than a doctrinal principle only to be cognitively known. It engages us in character formation. As Henri Nouwen's writings emphasize, it is one thing to know *about* Jesus or even to *know* Jesus and another to live as Jesus lived. It's perfectly possible for all of us to talk a good game about Jesus as opposed to living like him. Have we, though, dropped our masks? Do we know integrity of self? When people bump into us with impatience or anger, what spills out from us? Whom do they meet?

Ignatian spirituality offers one valuable perspective on humility. Ignatius identified three stages to this virtue. The first, evident at our conversion, involves a turning from naive trust in our power or in the world's power as sources of life. We renounce our autonomy and surrender to God. This remains an existentially profound move, not least in a culture of entitlement and false expectation. Thankfully, evangelicals are generally good at this initial stage of self-abandonment and submission.

In the first stage, Jesus does 'not consider equality with God something to be grasped'. However, in the second stage he goes beyond this and makes himself nothing. The one who would ultimately ascend to the Father's right hand comes to us as a servant. I recently discussed this paradox with a spiritual director. He illustrated the mystery of Jesus' dual nature in concrete form on the windowsill behind me. There an icon depicted Christ as the ascended King, resplendent on his throne, receiving the worship of angels. Next to this icon, though, stood a sculpture of Jesus washing a disciple's feet. Jesus is both enthroned King and foot-washer. In the second stage of humility, we seek to become more like Jesus the servant, the one who makes himself nothing. Evangelicals emphasize our personal relationship with God but, perhaps, less this 'descending' discipleship and spirituality of transformation.

The second Ignatian stage of humility entails increasing demands. We see this in the spiritual boot camp in which Jesus schools his disciples. He identifies and challenges any attitude militating against Christlike service. Luke 9:46 typically and depressingly begins, 'An argument started among the disciples as to which of them would be the greatest.' Jesus counsels counter-intuitive motives to subvert the personal ego. We are to wait to be exalted by someone higher than us. We are to take the lowest place at the table rather than secure the privileged position. These are less death blows than a constant whittling process. They will always, though, be offensive to our flesh.

I remember visiting Trinity College, Bristol, as a potential theological college for study when considering ordination. As

I was struggling to accept this call, the smell of boiled cabbage in the corridors and prospect of a return to school assaulted me physically. I left the college with my wife and was heartily sick in the gutter. Humility can do a necessary violence to our character. By contrast, we see humility embodied in Nelson Mandela, a man utterly grounded in who he was. Jessie Duarte, Deputy Secretary General of the ANC, testifies how Mandela insisted on making his own bed wherever he travelled. At the risk of offending the chambermaids in his Shanghai hotel by doing so, Mandela insisted that the hotel manager bring them to his room so that he could explain himself and ensure they did not feel insulted. Duarte observes: 'He never really cared about what great big people think of him, but he did care about what small people thought of him.'[8]

In this second stage, humility does not emerge spontaneously but is the fruit of intentional formation. Pope Francis is, for believers and many non-believers alike, a model of humility. Yet appointed as the head of the Jesuits in Argentina and Uruguay in 1973, Jorge Mario Bergoglio (now Pope Francis) initially led in a way that proved autocratic, controversial and divisive. Exiled in 1990 by the Jesuits as punishment to Cordoba, four hundred miles from Argentina's capital, Bergoglio was forced to turn inwards and reflect on his previous leadership. Permitted only to work on his doctoral thesis and to hear confession, he was not able to preside at Mass in public, he had his letters controlled, and he could only make phone calls with official permission. Father Guillermo Marco, later Bergoglio's right-hand man on public affairs in Buenos Aires, attests: 'Cordoba was, for Bergoglio, a place of humility and humiliation.'[9] Bergoglio himself, in his first interview as Pope, said that the Cordoba years were 'a time of great interior crisis'[10] and, later, that he made literally 'hundreds of errors' in his former leadership.[11]

By the time of his return to Buenos Aires as an auxiliary bishop in 1992, Bergoglio had completely remodelled his leadership approach. He now led through consultation and always ended private meetings by asking the other person to pray for him. In short, humility was never an innate part of his character but a consciously courted strategy to undermine his egotistical traits. So, in the second stage of humility, we too agree to become nothing, laying ourselves aside. Humility gradually becomes a natural expression and joy, but only through carefully cultivated practice.

Bergoglio's story exemplifies a godly response to life's setbacks and failures that propel us involuntarily along the paschal path. Bergoglio always sought to understand his exile within the framework of God's sovereignty, commenting on his painful exile:

> I cannot say that I have been wronged, although others believe it. A religious should never say: 'I suffered an injustice', because he must always find within himself, in all cases and under all circumstances, the path of God, the way to an inner purification.[12]

Bergoglio could have camped out bitterly at this place of apparent ministry humiliation. He didn't. He chose to ask – God, how are you present in this? What new thing are you calling me into? He allowed himself to suffer a death. More than a decade after Bergoglio's return from exile, a politician who had just lost an election and was feeling rejection approached him for words of advice. Bergoglio replied: 'Live your exile. I lived mine. And afterwards you will be back. And when you do come back you, you will be more merciful, kinder, and will want to serve your people better.'[13] Nothing goes away until it teaches us what it wants us to know.

In the third stage of humility, we descend further at greatest cost. We previously identified with Jesus in his incarnation and service. Now we unite with him in his descent to the lower depths. This stage correlates to the paschal journey from Gethsemane in which Jesus 'humbled himself and became obedient to death – even death on a cross'. Having graduated in humility's first two stages, we now accompany Jesus on this Calvary road. We share with him in his sufferings. We develop an affinity with moments in his ministry where he experienced insult, rejection, suffering and death. We come to a new participation in the lives of the marginalized and the poor. We experience a radical opening of heart and a new birthing of compassion. Above all, we remain intimately bound to Jesus in the face of opposition.

Jean Vanier, a Canadian diplomat's son and philosophy professor, who moved into a French house with two men with learning difficulties, thus birthing the community of L'Arche, comments: 'Humility is to enter into a relationship with people who have been humiliated. It's a beautiful way to learn how to live the Gospel message.'[14] Henri Nouwen similarly abandoned an Ivy League teaching career to join Vanier on this path. The persecuted church is populated with saints who identify with Jesus' love in the place of suffering. At the same time, we must remember not to cast humility with a self-destructive gloss. In its third stage, humility is never about courting suffering or death. It is the product of a devoted, joyful cleaving to Christ. It involves realistic acceptance that helping others or speaking out God's life-giving truth may come at a cost. Supremely, it stems from a continuing commitment to follow the one who is love.

Growth into this third paschal stage of humility will always be profoundly challenging. It involves both intentionality and abandonment. Spiritual directors Coombs and Nemeck, discussing our preparation for personal death itself, describe this duality:

> Are we active or passive in death? Is death something that we do or is it done to us? The response is: both. Obviously, death is primarily something that happens to us. We undergo it. Yet there really is something that we must do in our death. We do die. We let our whole self die. We let it happen lovingly, knowingly, willingly.[15]

We assent to the process of spiritual dying and growth but also submit to a larger process and allow God and his angels to carry us across these thresholds. We travel to a borderland's edge and discover that the Holy Spirit helps us 'pass over'. Graced by the Spirit in this way, we discover fullness of life. Charismatics sometimes speak of 'getting hold' of the power of the Holy Spirit. However, the nineteenth-century Baptist preacher A. J. Gordon provides necessary perspective:

> We should abandon the idea that we are to use the Holy Ghost, and to accept the thought that the Holy Ghost is to use us. There is a wide distinction between those two conceptions. I was in the Chicago World's Fair, and was attracted to a man dressed up in a very gaudy Oriental costume, who was turning with all his might a crank which was attached to a pump from which a great stream of water was pouring out. I said, 'That man is working hard and producing splendid results.' I came near and, to my astonishment, found that the man which was really only wooden, was not turning the crank, but the crank was turning him and, instead of his making that stream of water go, it was making him go. Many people want the secret of power. They hear about Peter preaching that wonderful sermon and of course they would give anything if they had the ability to preach one sermon and convert three

> thousand people. They say to Peter, 'How did you get hold of that power?' 'I didn't get hold of the power at all', he would say; 'the power got hold of me' . . . As a wheel dips itself into the river and makes all the cotton factories whirl, so Peter dipped into the Spirit and was swept by the current.[16]

How did Peter become receptive to the Holy Spirit's seizing? By relinquishing grandiosity, travelling the humble path, and coming to ground. He ceased to see himself as exalted. He chose to see himself as the limited but faithful follower of Jesus who had always been saved by grace and would accomplish nothing further except in his weakness and through God's strength. Peter had travelled all of the paschal cycle's stages and been broken and reshaped by the limitless grace of God. As a result, he could align himself to Jesus in any personal future Gethsemane. He could agree to be led where he did not want to go. Finally, in the future, facing crucifixion, he would ask to be crucified upside down, feeling unworthy of dying as Jesus did. Peter had embraced humility. Giving himself away in life and death, he helped birth the early church.

The three central lessons of the paschal narrative, then, are: know the story which you inhabit; travel that story closely with others; and emulate Jesus' humble obedience to God's larger purposes. It is possible to attempt to navigate life without the paschal map, as many people do in our fractured world. However, immersion in this mystery not only schools us in the complex dynamics of human change. It leads us into the truth of God's abiding love and into fullness of life. We discover that we are held, sustained and blessed, however opaque or fractured life seems to be in any moment.

Moreover, this is not a journey with an end. As the paschal journey involves increasing identification with, and participation in, Christ, so we will long for the return of the King.

We will ache for his second coming. In the words of the angels to the disciples: 'This same Jesus, who has been taken from you into heaven, will come back in the same way you have seen him go into heaven' (Acts 1:11). The angels reveal that this transformation cycle will continue into eternity. The early church expressed their longing for this in the yearning prayer 'Maranatha' ('O Lord, come') of Revelation 22:20. Charles Spurgeon opined: 'I believe that the Second Advent of Christ may be used as a thermometer with which to tell the degree of our spiritual heat.'[17] The second coming has often been central to revival preaching. In the Lowestoft Revival, Douglas Brown spoke for fifty minutes on thirty-one consecutive afternoons about the personal return of Christ. He later reported that the many conversions were 'largely through the preaching of the truth of the Lord's coming'.[18] We might say that just as the Holy Spirit points back to Jesus' saving work on the cross, he also points forward to Christ's imminent return. Biblically grounded discipleship does not end in the outward-faced mission of Acts but involves our thirsting to meet Jesus face to face. As St John says, 'we know that when he appears, we shall be like him, for we shall see him as he is' (1 John 3:2). 'Maranatha' was not just to be the prayer of early Christians who had greater immediate cause to expect Christ's imminent return. It is to be the prayer of any believer who longs for the sweetness of an age when 'there will be no more death or mourning or crying or pain' and we will gaze on Jesus at last (Revelation 21:4). The second letter of Peter implies that our active yearning for his return may even accelerate this reality ('as you look forward to the day of God and speed its coming', 3:12).

C. S. Lewis pictured Jesus diving into the seabed's 'death-like regions' to pluck us out and lift us up to heavenly places. This thrilling image evokes Christ's incarnation and ascension.

Bonhoeffer applies a similar image of descent and liberation to Jesus' second coming. At that time, he says that there will be joy in only one place on earth:

> That place is the congregation of Christ's people. They know he comes to redeem them. They are like miners who have been shut up in the depths of the mine, who have suffered long, shut up in the dark, who hear the knocking and the breaking down of walls coming closer. Is it the final caving-in of the mine or is the rescuer coming? . . . The earth, its suffering and temptation, makes us anxious, but Christ makes us glad, he brings redemption.[19]

Revelation 21 – 22 describes an age when, freed from shadowy confinement in the 'now' and 'not yet', we will know heaven and earth co-joined and impregnating one another. St John in his vision no longer sees a temple because 'the Lord God Almighty and the Lamb are its temple' (21:22). All creation is shot through with God's presence. Every person worships God-on-earth, enjoying perfect communion with him.

In case we think, as our sceptical culture often mocks, that this will involve an eternity of monotonous worship and satiated desire, let us note the view of twelfth-century reformer Bernard of Clairvaux. In Bernard, we have a supreme chronicler of spiritual desire and its role in Christian discipleship. He envisions eternity in a thrilling way, one combining perfect joy and an endless revitalizing of desire:

> God is sought not on foot but by desire. And the happy discovery of what is desired does not end desire but extends it. The consummation of joy does not consume desire, does it? Rather it is oil poured on flames, which itself catches fire. Thus it is. Joy will be fulfilled (Psalm 15:11). But there will no end to desire, and so no end of seeking.[20]

The paschal narrative illuminates the earthly cycle of transformation in which we become united in Christ. Yet here Bernard reminds us that this pattern of transformation will not be confined to earth. His incandescent imagery suggests that our cup will be filled in heaven and will continue to be enlarged for our ongoing receiving. Mystery of mysteries, our journey of growth in Christ will be unending.

After the descent of Jesus' earthly ministry, the end of the Philippians 2 hymn reveals the consummation of God's sovereign plan in Christ's exaltation:

> Therefore God exalted him to the highest place
>   and gave him the name that is above every name,
> that at the name of Jesus every knee should bow,
>   in heaven and on earth and under the earth,
> and every tongue confess that Jesus Christ is Lord,
>   to the glory of God the Father.
> (Philippians 2:9–11)

We shall see this universal bowing of knees to Christ at his second coming and final judgment. At that time, we will be a people transfigured. In John Stott's words, 'we will glow forever with the glory of Christ.'[21] We will have progressed far beyond the surface panaceas for personal modification offered by our culture. Instead, God will make all things new. His glory will be visible in saved and sanctified beings dwelling in resurrection bodies charged with glory. We shall look back at the paschal narrative as the collective memory of how we came to be here in eternity. For now, though, on this side of that threshold, it is no memory but our present reality. Living into it here and now, we can begin to relish the astonishing abundance of what is to come.

Notes

1 Introduction

1. F. W. Boreham, 'The Candle and the Bird', in *Boulevards of Paradise* (London: Epworth Press, 1944), p. 105.
2. Richard H. Schmidt, *Glorious Companions: Five Centuries of Anglican Spirituality* (Grand Rapids, MI: Eerdmans, 2002), p. 68.
3. You can see this sculpture at <www.tate.org.uk/art/archive/items/tga-8716-102/photographer-unknown-photograph-of-lazarus-by-jacob-epstein>.
4. William Bridges, *The Way of Transition* (Cambridge, MA: Da Capo Press, 2001), p. 8.
5. Bridges, *The Way of Transition*, p. 86.
6. Ronald Rolheiser, *The Holy Longing* (New York: Bantam Doubleday Dell Publishing Group, 2014).
7. Rebecca Solnit, *A Field Guide to Getting Lost* (Edinburgh: Canongate, 2006), p. 81.
8. Brenee Brown, 'The Power of Vulnerability' (TED talk, 2010), available at <www.ted.com/talks/brene_brown_on_vulnerability/transcript?quote=867#t-24289>.

2 Called

1. Martin Luther King, 'Speech at the Great March on Detroit' (23 June 1963), available at <http://kingencyclopedia.stanford.

edu/encyclopedia/documentsentry/doc_speech_at_the_great_march_on_detroit/index.html>.

2. Ingrid Hansen, *The Dark Night of the Soul: Growing in the Season of Loss* (Ingrid Hansen, 2012), pp. 13–14.
3. John O'Donohue, 'The Inner Landscape of Beauty' (radio interview, *On Being*, 2008), available at <https://onbeing.org/programs/john-odonohue-the-inner-landscape-of-beauty>.
4. Hansen, *The Dark Night of the Soul*, p. 14.
5. Belden Lane, *The Solace of Fierce Landscapes: Exploring Desert and Mountain Spirituality* (Oxford: Oxford University Press, 2007), p. 231.
6. Hansen, *The Dark Night of the Soul*, p. 13.
7. John Leach, *Survival Psychology* (Basingstoke: Palgrave Macmillan, 1994), pp. 166–167.
8. Stanley Griffin, *A Forgotten Revival* (Leominster: Day One Publications, 2001), pp. 16–17.
9. Griffin, *A Forgotten Revival*, p. 17.
10. Griffin, *A Forgotten Revival*, p. 17.
11. Griffin, *A Forgotten Revival*, p. 17.
12. Griffin, *A Forgotten Revival*, p. 17.
13. Leach, *Survival Psychology*, p. 160.
14. Eric Metaxas, *Bonhoeffer: Pastor, Martyr, Prophet, Spy* (Nashville, TN: Thomas Nelson, 2011), p. 321.
15. Metaxas, *Bonhoeffer*, pp. 339–340.
16. Metaxas, *Bonhoeffer*, p. 345.
17. Metaxas, *Bonhoeffer*, p. 345.
18. Metaxas, *Bonhoeffer*, p. 345.
19. Ian McEwan, *On Chesil Beach* (London: Vintage Books, 2008), p. 6.
20. McEwan, *On Chesil Beach*, p. 96.
21. McEwan, *On Chesil Beach*, pp. 139–40.
22. McEwan, *On Chesil Beach*, p. 166.
23. McEwan, *On Chesil Beach*, p. 166.

24. McEwan, *On Chesil Beach*, p. 165.
25. Greg Levoy, *Callings* (New York: Three Rivers Press, 1998), p. 271.
26. Leach, *Survival Psychology*, p. 172.
27. David Whyte, *The Heart Aroused* (London: Spiro Press, 2002), pp. 47–52.
28. Terry Eagleton, *Reason, Faith and Revolution* (New Haven, CT: Yale University Press, 2009), p. 27.

3 Crushed

1. Marie de Hennezel, *Seize the Day* (London: Macmillan, 2012), p. 18.
2. Oswald Chambers, *My Utmost for His Highest* (Grand Rapids, MI: Discovery House Publishers, 2005), p. 9.
3. A. W. Tozer, *The Classic Works of A. W. Tozer* (CreateSpace, 2013), p. 107.
4. Tim Urban, 'Why Generation Y Yuppies are Unhappy', *Wait But Why*, 9 September 2013, available at <https://waitbutwhy.com/2013/09/why-generation-y-yuppies-are-unhappy.html>.
5. W. H. Vanstone, *The Stature of Waiting* (London: Darton, Longman and Todd, 1982), p. 89.
6. De Hennezel, *Seize the Day*, p. xvi.
7. Parker J. Palmer, *Let Your Life Speak* (San Francisco, CA: Jossey-Bass, 2000), p. 32.
8. Palmer, *Let Your Life Speak*, p. 32.
9. You can see this painting at <https://en.wikipedia.org/wiki/Crucifixion_of_Saint_Peter_(Caravaggio)>.
10. Antoine Leiris, 'Bataclan Victim's Husband Tells Killers: "You Will Not Have My Hatred"', *The Guardian*, 17 November 2015, available at <www.theguardian.com/world/2015/nov/17/bataclan-paris-victim-helene-muyal-husband-antoine-leiris-killers-open-letter>.

11. De Hennezel, *Seize The Day*, p. 18.
12. Augustine, 'Sermo Suppositus', 120:3, quoted in Brant Pitre, *Jesus the Bridegroom* (New York: Image, 2014), p. 93.
13. Thomas Chalmers, 'The Expulsive Power of a New Affection', available at <https://www.monergism.com/expulsive-power-new-affection>.
14. Dietrich Bonhoeffer, *The Cost of Discipleship* (London: SCM Press, 2015), p. 44.
15. Phil Cousineau, *The Art of Pilgrimage* (Berkeley, CA: Conari Press, 1998), p. 110.
16. George Steiner, *Real Presences* (London: Faber and Faber, 2010), p. 267.

4 Buried

1. George Steiner, *Real Presences* (London: Faber and Faber, 2010), p. 267.
2. Rebecca Solnit, *A Field Guide to Getting Lost* (Edinburgh: Canongate, 2006), p. 83.
3. John Paul II, *Evangelium Vitae*, 25 March 1995, available at <http://w2.vatican.va/content/john-paul-ii/en/encyclicals/documents/hf_jp-ii_enc_25031995_evangelium-vitae.html>.
4. Matthew Arnold, *Dover Beach and Other Poems* (Mineola, NY: Dover Publications, 2000), p. 87.
5. Steiner, *Real Presences*, p. 267.
6. Ian McEwan, *On Chesil Beach* (London: Vintage Books, 2008), p. 163.
7. Marie de Hennezel, *Seize the Day* (London: Macmillan, 2012), p. 135.
8. Ralph Ellison, *Invisible Man* (New York: Vintage Books, 1980), p. 573.
9. John Stott, *The Cross of Christ* (Downers Grove, IL: InterVarsity Press, 2009), p. 72 (italics in original).

10. Peter Kreeft, *Jesus Shock* (Boston, MA: Beacon Publishing, 2008), p. 61.
11. Rebecca Solnit, *A Field Guide to Getting Lost* (Edinburgh: Canongate, 2006), pp. 82–83.
12. William Bridges, *Transitions* (Cambridge, MA: Da Capo Press, 2004), p. 41.
13. Heiner Stachelhaus, *Joseph Beuys* (New York: Abbeville Press Publishers, 1991), p. 48.
14. Stachelhaus, *Joseph Beuys*, pp. 52–53.
15. Mother Teresa, *Come: Be My Light*, ed. Brian Kolodiejchuk (New York: Doubleday, 2007), p. 214.
16. Mother Teresa, *Come*, p. 214.
17. C. S. Lewis, *The Screwtape Letters* (New York: Bantam Books, 1995), p. 24.
18. Shakespeare, *The Tempest*, Act 1, Scene 2.

5 Breathed on

1. Ronald Rolheiser, 'On the Road to Emmaus', 1 April 1984, available at <http://ronrolheiser.com/on-the-road-to-emmaus/#.WdscgUyZMdU>.
2. Rebecca Solnit, *A Field Guide to Getting Lost* (Edinburgh: Canongate, 2006), p. 22.
3. Andre Muller, 'Joseph Beuys', *Interviews* (Hamburg, 1982), p. 58.
4. C. S. Lewis, *The Lion, the Witch and the Wardrobe* (London: Collins, 1998), p. 170.
5. Charles Spurgeon, 'The Wounds of Jesus', sermon preached on 30 January 1859, p. 7, available at <http://archive.spurgeon.org/sermons/0254.php>.
6. Joseph Beuys, *Show Your Wound*, 1974–5. For more information, see <www.tate.org.uk/art/artworks/beuys-show-your-wound-ar00093>.
7. Geoff Dyer, *Zona* (Edinburgh: Canongate, 2012), p. 58.

8. William Bridges, *Transitions* (Cambridge, MA: Da Capo Press, 2004), p. 139.
9. Solnit, *A Field Guide to Getting Lost*, p. 22.
10. Solnit, *A Field Guide to Getting Lost*, pp. 6–7.
11. Rolheiser, 'On the Road to Emmaus'.
12. Bill Johnson and Jennifer Miskov, *Defining Moments* (New Kensington, PA: Whitaker House, 2016), p. 169.
13. Johnson and Miskov, *Defining Moments*, p. 169.
14. You can see this painting at <https://en.wikipedia.org/wiki/Crucifixion_of_Saint_Peter_(Caravaggio)>.
15. Walter Brueggemann, Question and Answer session of 'The Emergent Theological Conversation', Atlanta, Georgia, 16 September 2004, available at <https://onedaringjew.wordpress.com/2012/01/27/certainty-and-fidelity-in-biblical-interpretation-the-deconstruction-of-walter-brueggemann>.
16. Esther de Waal, *Living on the Border* (Norwich: Canterbury Press, 2011), p. 87.

6 Shaken

1. William Bridges, *The Way of Transition* (Cambridge, MA: Da Capo Press, 2001), p. 156.
2. Ingrid Hansen, *The Dark Night of the Soul: Growing in the Season of Loss* (Ingrid Hansen, 2012), p. 99.
3. Leonard Cohen, 'Credo', *The Spice Box of Earth* (London: Jonathan Cape, 1973), p. 30.
4. Bridges, *The Way of Transition*, p. 156.
5. William Bridges, *Transitions* (Cambridge, MA: Da Capo Press, 2004), p. xii.
6. Marie de Hennezel, *Seize the Day* (London: Macmillan, 2012), p. 130.
7. David Whyte, *Crossing the Unknown Sea* (New York: Riverhead Books, 2001), pp. 43, 46.

8. Ronald Rolheiser, *The Passion and the Cross* (Cincinnati, OH: Franciscan Media, 2015), p. 100.
9. David Whyte, *The Three Marriages* (New York: Riverhead Books, 2009), p. 263.
10. Charles Dickens, *Great Expectations* (London: Vintage, 2008), p. 460.
11. Laurence Gonzales, *Deep Survival* (New York: W. W. Norton and Co., 2004), p. 86.
12. Gonzales, *Deep Survival*, p. 169.
13. Gonzales, *Deep Survival*, p. 238.
14. Victor Turner, *The Ritual Process* (London: Routledge and Kegan Paul, 1969), p. 95.
15. Bruce Milne, *The Message of John* (Leicester: InterVarsity Press, 1993), commentary on John 21.
16. Hansen, *The Dark Night of the Soul*, p. 5.
17. David Whyte, 'The Sun', in *The House of Belonging* (Langley, WA: Many Rivers Press, 1996), p. 90.
18. This quotation is often mistakenly attributed to Anais Nin. It was written by Elizabeth Appell. See <http://anaisninblog.skybluepress.com/2013/03/who-wrote-risk-is-the-mystery-solved>.
19. Belden Lane, *The Solace of Fierce Landscapes: Exploring Desert and Mountain Spirituality* (New York: Oxford University Press, 2007), p. 230.
20. Andrew Jones, *Pilgrimage* (Abingdon: Bible Reading Fellowship, 2011), pp. 33–34.
21. Paul Tillich, *The Shaking of the Foundations* (Eugene, OR: Wipf and Stock, 2012), p. 156.
22. Sigmund Freud, *Complete Psychological Works of Sigmund Freud, Volume 11* (London: Vintage Classics, 2001), p. 199.

7 Blessed

1. Ronald Rolheiser, *Sacred Fire: A Vision for a Deeper Humanity and Christian Maturity* (New York: Image Books, 2014), p. 310.

2. Ernesto Cardenal, *The Gospel in Solentiname* (Maryknoll, NY: Orbis Books, 2010), p. 511.
3. C. S. Lewis, *The Joyful Christian* (New York: Simon and Schuster, 1996), pp. 54–55.
4. Andrew Murray, 'August 30', in *Daily Thoughts on Holiness* (Fort Washington, PA: CLC Publications, 2011).
5. Abraham Kuyper, *Abraham Kuyper: A Centennial Reader* (Grand Rapids, MI: Eerdmans, 1998), p. 461.
6. Henri Nouwen, *Life of the Beloved* (Chicago, IL: Independent Publishers Group, 2002), p. 117.
7. David Whyte, *Crossing the Unknown Sea* (New York: Riverhead Books, 2001), p. 47.
8. Laurence Gonzales, *Deep Survival* (New York: W. W. Norton and Co., 2004), p. 189.
9. Nouwen, *Life of the Beloved*, p. 120.
10. Rolheiser, *Sacred Fire*, p. 214.
11. Margaret Silf, *Sacred Spaces: Stations on a Celtic Way* (Oxford: Lion Publishing, 2001), p. 181.
12. David Whyte, *River Flow: New and Selected Poems 1984–2007* (Langley, WA: Many Rivers Press, 2007), pp. 104–105.
13. Heiner Stachelhaus, *Joseph Beuys* (New York: Abbeville Press Publishers, 1991), p. 53.
14. David Whyte, *A Great Invitation* (Langley, WA: Many Rivers Press, 2013), audio CD.
15. Charles Williams, *Essential Writings in Spirituality and Theology* (Eugene, OR: Wipf and Stock Publishers, 2016), p. 60.

8 Begging

1. Karl Barth, *Evangelical Theology* (Edinburgh: T. & T. Clark, 1979), p. 58.
2. Leonard Ravenhill, *Why Revival Tarries* (Minneapolis, MN: Bethany House, 2004), p. 19.

3. Ronald Rolheiser, 'Pentecost Happened at a Meeting', 26 January 2003, available at <http://ronrolheiser.com/pentecost-happened-at-a-meeting/#.WdvTcEyZP-Y>.
4. Bertha Chambers, *Oswald Chambers: His Life and Work* (Eugene, OR: Wipf and Stock, 2017), pp. 46–47.
5. Alan Jamieson, *Chrysalis: The Hidden Transformation in the Journey of Faith* (Milton Keynes: Paternoster, 2007), p. 54.
6. Arnold Toynbee, *A Study of History: Abridgement of Volumes 1–6* (New York: Oxford University Press, 1988), p. 217.
7. I am indebted to my colleague Simon Ponsonby for these insights about the presence of the women in the upper room.
8. Simon Ponsonby, *God is for Us: 52 Readings from Romans* (Oxford: Monarch Books, 2013), p. 437.
9. Victor Turner, *The Ritual Process* (London: Routledge and Kegan Paul, 1969), pp. 96–97, 128.
10. Leonard Hjalmarson, 'Forty Years in a Narrow Space', available at <http://nextreformation.com/wp-admin/resources/liminal.pdf>.
11. Charles Spurgeon, 'Prayer Meetings', sermon preached on 27 August 1859, p. 4, available at <www.spurgeongems.org/vols58-60/chs3421.pdf>.
12. Spurgeon, 'Prayer Meetings', p. 4.
13. Colin and Mary Peckham, *Sounds from Heaven* (Fearn: Christian Focus, 2011), p. 202.
14. Rolheiser, 'Pentecost Happened at a Meeting'.
15. Spurgeon, 'Prayer Meetings'.
16. Charles Finney, *Lectures on Revivals of Religion* (New York: Leavitt, Lord and Co., 1835), p. 26.
17. William Booth, *Visions* (Dickinson, ND: Revival Press, 2014), p. 126.
18. Arthur Wallis, *In the Day of Thy Power* (Washington, PA: CLC Publications, 1956), p. 138.
19. Peckham, *Sounds from Heaven*, p. 131.
20. Peckham, *Sounds from Heaven*, p. 112.

21. Brian H. Edwards, *Revival!* (Darlington: Evangelical Press, 1990), p. 75.
22. Edwards, *Revival!*, p. 257.
23. Simon Ponsonby, *More* (Colorado Springs, CO: David C. Cook, 2010), p. 146.
24. Ernest Baker, *The Revivals of the Bible* (Greenville, SC: Emerald House Group, 1971), p. 30.
25. Edwards, *Revival!*, p. 79.
26. Lewis Hyde, *The Gift: How the Creative Spirit Transforms the World* (Edinburgh: Canongate Books, 2007), pp. 145–146.
27. A. J. Gordon, 'Fifty Eight A. J. Gordon Quotations', p. 5, available at <www.biblesnet.com/AJ%20Gordon%20Fifty%20Eight%20A.%20J.%20Gordon%20Quotations.pdf>.
28. Raymond Edman, *They Found the Secret* (Grand Rapids, MI: Zondervan, 1984), p. 53.
29. Charles Finney, 'Revival Born in a Prayer Meeting', in *Knowing & Doing* (Fall 2004), reprinted from *America's Great Revivals* (Minneapolis, MN: Bethany House Publishers).

9 Filled

1. Søren Kierkegaard, *Provocations: Spiritual Writings of Kierkegaard* (Farmington, PA: Plough, 1999), pp. xix, 334.
2. James Stuart Stewart, *Heralds of God* (Grand Rapids, MI: Baker Book House, 1972), p. 219.
3. Samuel Chadwick, *The Way to Pentecost* (CreateSpace, 2016), p. 13.
4. Hudson Taylor, quoted in *Ecumenical Missionary Conference*, Volume 1 (New York: American Tract Society, 1900), p. 88.
5. Lewis Hyde, *The Gift: How the Creative Spirit Transforms the World* (Edinburgh: Canongate Books, 2007), p. 146.
6. Ronald Rolheiser, *The Passion and the Cross* (Cincinnati, OH: Franciscan Media, 2015), p. 66.

7. Maria Theresa Coombs and Francis Kelly Nemeck, *The Spiritual Journey* (Collegeville, MN: Liturgical Press, 1986), p. 20.
8. Rebecca Solnit, *A Paradise Built in Hell: The Extraordinary Communities that Arise in Disaster* (New York: Viking, 2009), p. 66.
9. Raymond Edman, *They Found the Secret* (Grand Rapids, MI: Zondervan, 1984), p. 29.
10. Smith Wigglesworth, *Faith that Prevails* (Radford, VA: Wilder Publications, 2008), p. 27.
11. Wigglesworth, *Faith that Prevails*, p. 27.
12. C. S. Lewis, *The Voyage of the Dawn Treader* (London: Collins, 1998), pp. 113–119.
13. Tom Smail, *Reflected Glory* (London: Hodder and Stoughton, 1975), p. 105.
14. Blaise Pascal, *Thoughts* (Cambridge: Cambridge University Press, 2013), p. 218.
15. Edman, *They Found the Secret*, p. 55.
16. Edman, *They Found the Secret*, p. 55.
17. Raniero Cantalamessa, *Sober Intoxication of the Spirit: Filled with the Fullness of God* (Cincinnati, OH: Franciscan Media, 2005).
18. Stanley Griffin, *A Forgotten Revival* (Leominster: Day One Publications, 2001), p. 17.
19. Griffin, *A Forgotten Revival*, p. 17.
20. Griffin, *A Forgotten Revival*, p. 18.
21. Duncan Campbell, *Revival in the Hebrides* (CreateSpace, 2016), p. 62.
22. David Whyte, *Crossing the Unknown Sea* (New York: Riverhead Books, 2001), p. 141.
23. Colin Whitaker, *Great Revivals* (Eastbourne: Kingsway Publications, 2005), p. 114.
24. Griffin, *A Forgotten Revival*, p. 58.
25. Chadwick, *The Way to Pentecost*, p. 123.

26. A. W. Tozer, 'How to be Filled with the Holy Spirit', sermon, available at <www.sermonindex.net/modules/newbb/viewtopic.php?topic_id=22632&forum=34>.
27. Tozer, 'How to be Filled with the Holy Spirit'.
28. Edman, *They Found the Secret*, p. 55.
29. Andrew Murray, *The Holiest of All* (Lulu.com, 2011), p. 168.
30. Murray, *The Holiest of All*, p. 200.
31. Rosalind Goforth, *Goforth of China* (Eugene, OR: Wipf and Stock, 2014), p. 197.
32. Friedrich Zundel, *The Awakening: One Man's Battle with Darkness* (Farmington, PA: Plough, 1999), p. 58.
33. Chadwick, *The Way to Pentecost*, p. 23.

10 Released

1. Raymond Edman, *They Found the Secret* (Grand Rapids, MI: Zondervan, 1984), p. 77.
2. Edman, *They Found the Secret*, p. 101.
3. You can see this painting at <https://en.wikipedia.org/wiki/The_Light_of_the_World_(painting)>.
4. C. S. Lewis, quoted in Alister McGrath, *C. S. Lewis: Eccentric Genius, Reluctant Prophet* (Carol Stream, IL: Tyndale House, 2013), p. 140.
5. Paul Vallely, *Pope Francis: Untying the Knots* (London: Bloomsbury, 2015), p. 155.
6. John Wesley, quoted in Rosalind Brown and Christopher J. Cocksworth, *On Being a Priest Today* (New York: Rowman and Littlefield, 2004), p. 114.
7. David Frost, *Billy Graham: Candid Conversations with a Public Man* (Colorado Springs, CO: David C. Cook, 2014), pp. 69–70.
8. Timothy George, *Mr. Moody and the Evangelical Tradition* (London: Bloomsbury, 2005), p. 4.
9. Shakespeare, *Hamlet*, Act 5, Scene 2.

10. Eduard Thurneysen, *God's Search for Man: Sermons* (Edinburgh: T. & T. Clark, 1935), p. 72.
11. Dieter Ising, *Johann Christoph Blumhardt, Life and Work* (Eugene, OR: Wipf and Stock, 2009), p. 196.
12. Bill Johnson and Jennifer Miskov, *Defining Moments* (New Kensington, PA: Whitaker House, 2016), p. 88.
13. Kenneth Bailey, *Jesus through Middle Eastern Eyes: Cultural Studies in the Gospels* (Downers Grove, IL: InterVarsity Press, 2009), p. 182.
14. Frederick Buechner, *Listening to Your Life* (New York: HarperOne, 1992), p. 186.
15. James Buchan, *Frozen Desire* (London: Picador, 1998), p. 19.
16. Dorothy Rowe, *The Real Meaning of Money* (London: HarperCollins, 1998), p. xii.
17. C. S. Lewis, *Letters to an American Lady* (Grand Rapids, MI: Eerdmans, 2014), p. 13.
18. Robert Morris, *The Power of Your Words* (Harrisonburg, VA: Gospel Light Publications, 2009), p. 97.
19. Andrew Murray, *The Full Blessing of Pentecost* (Whitefish, MT: Kessinger Publishing 2008), p. 47.
20. Norman Grubb, *Rees Howells, Intercessor* (Cambridge: The Lutterworth Press, 2014), p. 30.
21. Tim Keller, *Generous Justice* (London: Hodder and Stoughton, 2010), p. 141.
22. Bernard Cooke and Gary Macy, *Christian Symbol and Ritual: An Introduction* (Oxford: Oxford University Press, 2005), p. 149.
23. Rebecca Solnit, *A Paradise Built in Hell: The Extraordinary Communities that Arise in Disaster* (London: Viking, 2009), p. 3.
24. Solnit, *A Paradise Built in Hell*, p. 3.
25. Solnit, *A Paradise Built in Hell*, p. 18.
26. Solnit, *A Paradise Built in Hell*, p. 208.

27. Jon Tyson and Heather Grizzle, *A Creative Minority: Influencing Culture through Redemptive Participation* (Heather Grizzle, 2016), p. 12.
28. Johnson and Miskov, *Defining Moments*, p. 169.
29. Johnson and Miskov, *Defining Moments*, pp. 182–183.
30. Duncan Campbell, 'The Price and Power of Revival', ch. 4, available at <www.gospeltruth.net/campbell/campbellchap4.htm>.
31. Philip Yancey and Paul Brand, *Fearfully and Wonderfully Made* (Grand Rapids, MI: Zondervan, 2010), p. 82.

11 Igniting

1. Elisabeth Elliot, *Through Gates of Splendor* (Carol Stream, IL: Tyndale Momentum, 1981), p. 18.
2. Charles Spurgeon, 'Who are the Elect?', sermon preached on 9 July 1865, p. 8, available at <www.spurgeongems.org/vols10-12/chs638.pdf>.
3. Smith Wigglesworth, *The Anointing of His Spirit* (Bloomington, MN: Chosen Books, 2014), p. 160.
4. Elliot, *Through Gates of Splendor*, p. 18.
5. Arthur Wallis, *In the Day of Thy Power* (Washington, PA: CLC Publications, 1956), p. 29.
6. F. F. Bruce, *The Spreading Flame* (London: Paternoster Press), 1964.
7. David Whyte, *Crossing the Unknown Sea* (New York: Riverhead Books, 2001), pp. 142–143.
8. John F. Wippel, *Metaphysical Themes in Thomas Aquinas II*, Volume 2 (Washington, DC: Catholic University of America Press, 2007), p. 141.
9. Samuel Chadwick, quoted in 'Samuel Chadwick Burned His Sermons and Caught Fire Himself!', available at <https://makinghistorynow.wordpress.com/2017/06/02/preacher-burns-his-sermons-and-catches-fire-himself>.

10. Samuel Chadwick, *The Way to Pentecost* (CreateSpace, 2016), p. 29.
11. William Barclay, *The Gospel of Luke* (Philadelphia, PA: Westminster John Knox Press, 1956), p. 92. The quotation has often been misattributed to G. K. Chesterton. See <https://fauxtations.wordpress.com/2014/12/17/chesterton-fearless-happy-and-in-constant-trouble>.
12. You can see this painting at <https://en.wikipedia.org/wiki/The_Stoning_of_Saint_Stephen>.
13. Ottar G. Draugsvold, *Nobel Writers on Writing* (Jefferson, NC: McFarland, 2000), p. 146.
14. Charles Spurgeon, 'Stephen's Death', sermon preached on 24 May 1874, p. 4, available at <www.spurgeongems.org/vols19-21/chs1175.pdf>.
15. Smith Wigglesworth, *The Anointing of His Spirit*, p. 161.
16. Nik Ripken, 'Biblical Lessons from the Persecuted Church', p. 3, available at <http://nikripken.com/wp-content/themes/nikripken/downloads/Biblical%20Lessons%20from%20the%20Persecuted%20Church.pdf>.
17. Pope Francis, 'Two Kinds of Persecution', Morning Meditation preached on 12 April 2016, available at <https://w2.vatican.va/content/francesco/en/cotidie/2016/documents/papa-francesco-cotidie_20160412_two-kinds-of-persecution.html>.
18. Dietrich Bonhoeffer, *The Cost of Discipleship* (London: SCM Press, 2015), p. 45.
19. Jonathan Goforth, *By My Spirit* (Createspace, 2015), ch. 5.
20. Goforth, *By My Spirit*, ch. 5.
21. Goforth, *By My Spirit*, ch. 5.
22. Carol Dingle, *Memorable Quotations: French Writers of the Past* (Bloomington, IN: iUniverse, 2000), p. 126.
23. Augustine, *Sermons (148–183): On the New Testament*, ed. John E. Rotelle, trans. Edmund Hill (New York: New City Press, 1992), p. 26.

12 Conclusion

1. F. W. Boreham, 'The Candle and the Bird', in *Boulevards Of Paradise* (London: Epworth Press, 1944), p. 113.
2. Charles Seymour Robinson, *The New Laudes Domini: A Selection of Spiritual Songs, Ancient and Modern* (New York: Century Company, 1892), p. 204.
3. W. K. Volmer, *These Things: A Reference Manual for Discipleship* (Lulu.com, 2016), p. 233.
4. Julian Barnes, *Nothing to be Frightened of* (London: Random House, 2008), pp. 189–190.
5. Marie de Hennezel, *Seize the Day* (London: Macmillan, 2012), p. 115.
6. Greg Levoy, *Callings* (New York: Three Rivers Press, 1998), p. 250.
7. Henri Nouwen, *The Return of the Prodigal Son* (New York: Image Books, 1994), p. 56.
8. Jessie Duarte, 'Interview: Jessie Duarte', available at <www.pbs.org/wgbh/pages/frontline/shows/mandela/interviews/duarte.html>.
9. Paul Vallely, *Pope Francis: Untying the Knots* (London: Bloomsbury, 2015), p. 53.
10. Vallely, *Pope Francis*, p. 114.
11. Vallely, *Pope Francis*, p. 84.
12. Vallely, *Pope Francis*, p. 113.
13. Vallely, *Pope Francis*, p. 125.
14. Jean Vanier, 'God Chooses the Despised', an interview from 5 August 2015, available at <www.americamagazine.org/content/all-things/god-chooses-despised-interview-2015-templeton-prize-laureate-jean-vanier>.
15. Maria Theresa Coombs and Francis Kelly Nemeck, *The Spiritual Journey* (Collegeville, MN: Liturgical Press, 1986), p. 224.

16. A. J. Gordon, 'Fifty Eight A. J. Gordon Quotations', p. 9, available at <www.biblesnet.com/AJ%20Gordon%20Fifty%20 Eight%20A.%20J.%20Gordon%20Quotations.pdf>.
17. Charles Spurgeon, 'Come, My Beloved!', sermon preached on 13 May 1894, p. 1, available at <www.spurgeongems.org/ ols40-42/chs2360.pdf>.
18. David W. Bebbington, *Evangelicalism in Modern Britain: A History from the 1730s to the 1980s* (London: Routledge, 2003), p. 192.
19. Edwin Robertson, *I Stand at the Door: The Advent Sermons of Dietrich Bonhoeffer* (Bath: Eagle Publishing, 2003), pp. 101–102.
20. G. R. Evans, *Bernard of Clairvaux: Selected Works* (New York: Paulist Press, 1987), p. 274.
21. John Stott, *The Gospel and the End of Time* (Downers Grove, IL: InterVarsity Press, 1991), p. 150.